ENDORSEME

A heart full of love that just simply wants to help, that's Donna! You can hear the heart of the Father minister His love for His children through the pages of this book! Help is on the way! Not just another read but an invitation to be free!

PAUL BRADY
President, Living Rivers USA

The very first time I met Donna I knew I was meeting someone who takes whatever she is given and maximizes the opportunity. This book and the journey of how it happened is a testimony of her character. When some saw COVID as an obstacle, she grabbed an opportunity; when some would stay unqualified, she determined to test what she knew about God, and the result is free people.

This book is needed right now, today! A generation is under attack in the mind and spirit, and we have what we need, but too few of us know how to access what we have. At the beginning of 2023, I began to sense a focus on mental health and freedom. This book is, I believe, a part of that. The range of issues this book covers—obesity, involvement in the occult, bullying and abuse, and the outcomes of ministry—embrace so much of what we need to see and experience today.

I can, as I often say, easily endorse a book so long as I agree, but the real pleasure is to endorse the book and the person. That is the case here. Donna is a person with great experience but who is also a learner. I love that and it comes through the narrative, giving confidence as we learn from someone who walks in the humility of lifelong learning. This book is real, raw, and relevant. The testimonies are inspiring, I almost wish there were before and after photos for each of the cases.

I love this introduction to the final chapter on testimonies:

> My sincere hope as you read this last chapter of the book is that it will just make sense, that the penny will drop, it has scratched the itch that you have never been able to reach! I am believing it has answered the questions that you have always been asking but could never resolve in your heart and mind. Ultimately, I am hoping this has helped you personally, especially if you have struggled in any of the areas discussed throughout this book. Be encouraged—there is hope and there is freedom!

This sums up the book and the hope that it gives. For all of us who call Jesus Lord, this book is an unpacking of the key of deliverance that opens the door into freedom for us and for those we may minister to. Read it, apply it, be changed, be free, and bring that to those you know, love, and serve.

PAUL MANWARING
Itinerant minister, coach, and strategist
Member of senior leadership team of Bethel Church,
Redding, CA
Author of *What on Earth Is Glory, Kisses from a Good God,
Things Fathers Do, Your Divine Purpose,* and
Encounter Christianity

Right now, the Spirit of God is at work to transform His churches into wombs of the spirit where mass deliverances can take place. Yet up until now, little has been understood about the delivering power of God, how it works, and who it is for.

This new book from Donna Howells is revelation in real time that is mission critical not only for the body of Christ at large, but for every person who calls themselves a Christ follower. The truths found in these pages are simple yet profound and can be immediately applied to your life. As you read it, you will discover a brand-new level of freedom you have never known. I am so excited for the release of this powerful new book, truly written for such a time as this.

REV. JEN TRINGALE
Jen Tringale Ministries
Speaker, author

I am convinced of the significance of this work from Donna Howells. It strikes me as an end-time guidebook to enlighten and refine the church. As a body we are called to be a church without spot or wrinkle, impervious to the wiles of the devil. Donna covers so many of the elements of weaponry, deliverance, and freedom that are needed for us to become the temple of the Lord, walking in complete victory over death!

KELLIE COPELAND
Kellie Copeland Ministries

Donna Howells, a dear friend and dedicated pastor, unveils the sinister realm of demonic oppression in *Devil, Come Out!* In this powerful book, she equips readers to recognize and ultimately conquer the forces that threaten to subdue our lives.

With unwavering faith, vulnerability, and profound insight, Donna's book is a beacon of hope in our battle against darkness. *Devil, Come Out!* is a must-read for anyone seeking to know more about or to reclaim their life from the grips of darkness.

Evangelist Andrew Cannon
Founder of Gospel Grenades
Author of *Dare to Share*

Devil, Come Out! is a great resource for every believer from every walk of life and every level of spiritual maturity. A book not just about demons but all about Jesus and the abundant life that He paid the high price for us to be living! As so powerfully outlined in this book, breaking free from the demonic limitations that seek to keep us bound up, blunt, and ineffective changes everything about your life and all that pertains to it! What an exciting adventure to embark on as you take hold of the truth and revelation within this book and become all that God intended for you!

It will enable you to break free from the cycles of destruction and dysfunction that become barriers to us walking out the fullness of God's original design for our lives. Free from darkness, demons, and works of the devil! Thank you, Pastor Donna Howells, for the powerful investment you have made into the Kingdom of God and the lives of all who read this book!

Dr. Brad Norman
Founder and Senior Pastor, SFTN Churches UK
Director, FaithUK TV

Devil, Come Out!

RECOGNIZE & DESTROY DEMONIC OPPRESSION IN YOUR LIFE

DONNA HOWELLS

DEDICATION

I AM SO GRATEFUL, FIRST AND FOREMOST, TO GOD THAT HE has allowed me even the smallest insight into this ministry we call deliverance. His trust in me to write this book blows me away every time I think about it.

Secondly, to all those who have helped me bring *Devil, Come Out!* to market, my heart is forever grateful to every one of you. From those who have sown finances, endorsed, fought in my corner, and prayed for this book to become a reality, thank you!

I also want to give a special mention and heartfelt thanks to Kyle, my publisher, and to Joseph and Heather Z; only the Lord knows the part you have played in producing this book.

Lastly, but by no means least, is my husband Robbie and my family—oh, my beautiful family—you guys are truly the best, and I love each one of you so much.

CONTENTS

FOREWORD

Donna Howells' new book, *DEVIL, COME OUT!*, speaks the truth about deliverance! Donna and her husband Robbie have experienced what real deliverance ministry is all about. This book is undoubtedly an eye-opener that ventures into the deliverance arena armed with a solid biblical foundation and birthed from a place of practice and discernment. The stories and testimonies are raw and straightforward, and the whole journey started because of one quasi-routine phone call.

Since my early years, I have encountered many people with dramatic stories and cases of deliverance, ranging from witches to regular people who dealt with demonic issues. Every demon came out in the name of Jesus. This book, however, deals with deliverance from a place of great sensitivity and honesty. Tough questions such as, "Can a Christian have a demon?" and more issues like it are addressed here—with clarity, I might add. Enlightening points are made by Donna as "deliverance of the saints" is a massive part of her ministry. She shows us that demons impact the souls of humanity, saved and unsaved alike, and knowing how to navigate this issue will be helpful for every reader.

As I read through the pages of this book, I found myself saying, "This is a well-rounded understanding of deliverance," and thought several times that Donna offers a healthy take on this issue. On each page, I found myself thinking about the matters Donna addresses as they are thought-provoking yet straightforward. The reader will find out that demons have personalities. They are wicked and evil spirits, and depending on the type of demon they are, their character traits will take over someone's personality without them even realizing it! You will then find out how to drive those evil spirits out!

Demons cannot stop the call of God on your life, but they can delay it by making it difficult for you to recognize that God has given you everything needed to accomplish what He has called you to do. Demons will do their best to make you content with living your Christian life without vision, victory, or true freedom in Christ. If the devil can't kill you, he will steal from you; if that doesn't work, he will try to destroy you. Maybe he can't take your life, but he will try and make your life a living hell while you're on earth, hoping you will turn away from God by losing all faith and trust in Him.

To combat the demonic influences we are facing at an all-time high, Donna unashamedly deals with real-world issues; she pulls back the cover on the kingdom of darkness and its wicked tactics and sheds light on the open doors by which the demonic attempts to access your life. It was refreshing to read how she skillfully deals with counseling and deliverance by showing that these two areas can work well together. She additionally made every instance she described understandable by conveying with transparency areas where these issues hit close to home.

What I found refreshing and encouraging about this book is the absence of learned religious overtones, but rather a significant level of biblical clarity and raw honesty. Here is a book that will assist anyone wanting to understand deliverance and utilize it as a step-by-step guide for operating in it.

Thank you to Donna for writing such a necessary and clear book on this vital subject! For many years to come, this book will be a source and point of reference on the topic of deliverance. I pray this written work finds itself in the right hands at the right time and that those who read this book find the answers they seek. Maybe the person I'm praying for is you. God bless you as you read *Devil, Come Out!*

JOSEPH Z
Author, broadcaster, prophetic voice
JosephZ.com

PREFACE

MY GOAL IN WRITING THIS BOOK IS TO BRING COMPLETE freedom to every believer. Everything that has ever weighed you down or slowed you down in your pursuit of the Lord—from your past to your present, from sin and shame, from guilt to fear. I believe this book will bring clarity of sight and understanding by revealing that deliverance is part of the salvation experience.

Before you read it, I want to preface it by saying that it is not a book about demon slaying. Neither is it about seeing a demon behind every bush! In fact, while the pages are full of stories, revelation, and keys to deal with the demonic realm, the whole point of this book is to present the reader with an answer they might not have realized they needed. We are promised in John 10:10 that Jesus came to give life and that life would be an abundant one. Too many believers are not living in the fulness of that promise, even though they know they should be. There are strongholds that believers have in their lives that will not shift no matter how many altar calls they respond to or how much fasting and praying they do. I believe that this book holds the missing key for many who cannot get free from those lifelong issues and struggles.

My hope for the reader is that this book will "just make sense." If this is you then, for some, it will be an emotional journey. There are subjects that I talk about that may remind you of everything you have tried to escape from. Years of suppressed thoughts, pushed-down feelings, battles with addictions, and emotions you hoped would eventually go away by themselves. It is like putting a band-aid on an open wound—it's only ever been a temporary fix. I believe this book has insight to bring complete healing, recovery, and restoration to every area of your life.

As a pastor, casting out demons is just part of what I do. It is not the main thing. It is, however, a very necessary part of the main thing, which is ultimately complete freedom in Christ. Sometimes when we receive a fresh revelation, we allow the pendulum to swing so far that we make it all about that one revelation or ministry. We must not allow that to happen. I believe that this is why the Lord entrusted me, my husband, my family, and my church with the anointing to walk in this ministry. We don't make it all about deliverance; we make it all about Jesus.

I want to encourage you—please don't misread or misinterpret what I have written. There are statements I make about physical, mental, or spiritual conditions that are demonic. However, I clearly show the reader that all of them have their *roots* in the demonic, but not everything is a demon. Please read this book with a heart to receive revelation that will help you personally or will enable you to minister to others. Not everyone will need the type of deliverance described in the pages of this book, but everyone should know that it is available to all those who call on the name of Jesus.

Some of the last words Jesus spoke to His disciples were that signs would follow them if they believed.

And these signs will follow those who believe: In My name they will cast out demons; they will speak with new tongues; they will take up serpents; and if they drink anything deadly, it will by no means hurt them; they will lay hands on the sick, and they will recover (Mark 16:17-18 NKJV).

Casting out demons was not separate to preaching the gospel—it was part of it. The gospel message brings redemption, healing, deliverance, and prosperity. This is the life that Jesus died for so that we could live. A life of abundance—body, soul, and spirit—for us to demonstrate through our own lives the good news of the gospel.

With all my heart, I am hoping you will embrace the message within this book. It has the potential to bring you healing and wholeness, freedom and power, all for the glory of God.

DONNA HOWELLS

CHAPTER 1

SEEDS
HEREDITARY CURSES AND BLOODLINES

IN MINISTERING DELIVERANCE TO PEOPLE, I INEVITABLY come to the same conclusion—messed-up adults are the result of messed-up childhoods. Whenever I sit down to listen to a person's story, I will always ask them to talk about their childhood as far back as they can remember. This is because for many people, going back is the only way for them to go forward. Family trauma, generational habits, or inherited genes can be responsible for the situation a person can find themselves in. If you go back far enough, there will always be a strategic moment in a person's past or family history that opened the door that set off a chain reaction of behavioral traits or destructive patterns in a family line. I call it a seed, and it's a seed of destruction planted by Satan which is responsible for mapping out a dysfunctional future of a family or generation without them even knowing it.

You will often find a pattern of behavior in a family's history that began way before the person you are ministering to was ever born. Certainly not all, but many of those who have received deliverance ministry have come from a family line where dysfunction has been at the core. I find it so interesting that very few people are aware of this type of strategy that Satan uses to manipulate and destroy people. It's not new to our generation; Satan has used this form of warfare on mankind from the beginning, and he has watched his handiwork play out throughout the history of the world.

We know that Satan is the great deceiver, but he is also the original manipulator! To manipulate is to cause a person to change the way they think in order to fit into a narrative that is against their own personal belief system, and it always has a detrimental effect on the person. Satan is the biggest manipulator on planet Earth, and it all started in the garden.

When we look in the book of Genesis, we can see that the first thing Satan did in the form of the serpent was to use deception and manipulation to trick Eve. He initially deceived her into thinking he was a serpent—why didn't he come as himself? Eve probably didn't realize she was talking to Satan, and had she realized it was the deceiver himself, there may never have been a conversation. Satan hid his true identity so that Eve would listen to what he had to say. He was also able to deceive and manipulate Eve into thinking God said something other than what He did say (wait for the manipulation!), in order to benefit his own wicked scheme. He twisted the truth of what God said in such a way that it sounded plausible to Eve—it actually sounded *like* God's voice. Let me just add this here—if you say you know God yet fail to recognize His voice, you will always be in danger of being deceived by the enemy!

The dictionary definition of *manipulate/manipulation* is "control or influence (a person or situation) cleverly or unscrupulously; to exploit, control, influence, maneuver, engineer, steer, direct; to alter or present (data) to mislead to falsify, rig, distort, change."

Satan did all the above and more! Every descriptive word for the definition of *manipulate* describes a personality trait that he has. In today's terminology, we may call it *gaslighting*, which means manipulating a person so that they question their own judgment or believe a lie they have continually been convinced is the truth. More significantly, Satan sowed a negative seed into Eve's mind about her heavenly Father, the Creator. It wasn't a good seed! He distorted the initial command God gave Adam to not eat from the tree of life, knowing that this would exploit, control, and influence Eve. The seed was sown at the commencement of his wicked plan to sever God's relationship with man. It started with a seed of destruction! A half-truth, a manipulation, a deception, yet a seed that would produce after its kind for generations to come. The seed was sown into the mind of Eve, and eventually Adam, but more crucially into both their hearts! The seed sown was "Did God say?" and the seed it produced was trust in oneself and pride in the heart (skepticism, suspicion, doubt, distrust concerning God). It was not just sown into the hearts of Adam and Eve but their family line and in the heart of the whole of creation from that moment until now.

When you look at a seed in the natural, let's say a flower seed, it is generally very small, but you know given the right environment and through the course of time, as you water it, something will eventually happen. The outer shell will crack and the life that is on the inside of the seed will start to expand

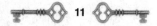

and grow; it will stretch out and embed itself into the surroundings it is planted in. When a seed is sown, good or bad, it always produces a multiplied amount of what it contained; it has the ability to produce and increase itself on an exponential level.

Let's go back to the dictionary and look at the definition for the word *destruction*: "the action or process of causing so much damage to something that it no longer exists or cannot be repaired."

I believe from the beginning of time Satan's number-one plan was to destroy and eradicate mankind from planet earth. He was incensed that God had made another creation greater than him and was probably jealous of Adam and Eve's status and the relationship that they had with God. He didn't quite manage to eradicate man, but he ended up destroying man's relationship with his Creator, which was far worse than death itself! Sowing seeds of destruction into the lives of God's creation to distort, alter, and change what God originally intended for man was a strategic plan of the enemy, the consequences of which have continued to this present day! That initial seed that had Eve questioning God's intention toward her is still operating in the heart of man. Many people are doubtful that a God who loves them unconditionally could even exist, let alone that He would have a plan or a purpose for them. This is all from a seed sown concerning God's motive by questioning, "Did God say?"

I discovered something recently which gave me that "aha" moment. Before I go into detail and explain, let's just establish a couple of facts—Satan cannot create anything. The only thing he can do is distort, pervert, and try to destroy what God has created. When God created man, He created him in His image

and then out of him He created her! Male and female, the only two genders that are possible biologically and scientifically. The way He created them was from the earth, first with Adam and then Eve from Adam's rib, so both came from the substance of the earth, and both were made in His image.

God is the greatest scientist to ever exist. We may think of incredible scientists in our history books, but they don't even compare to the knowledge and know-how that God has. The only reason we marvel at scientists today is because God chose to allow them to partake of His knowledge. Everything we are and have as humans comes from God. We are the image of Him. When God said to Jesus and the Holy Spirit in the beginning, "*Let Us make man in Our image, according to Our likeness*" (Genesis 1:26 NKJV), He wasn't only referring to physical appearance! God chose to pour everything He was and is into Adam and Eve. All His knowledge, all His know-how, all His love, all His ability, all His breath!

So let me get back to my "aha" moment! In delivering people, as I have previously said, the history of a person is everything. It's only by understanding where they have come from and what they have experienced that we can track down where the door first opened for Satan to gain access into their life.

As I was in the process of making some programs for an online Christian TV channel about Christians and the subject of sex, my daughter who was helping me with some of the research handed me her notes. What I read blew my mind! In trying to understand the addiction to pornography, she had come across a term called *epigenetics*. Epigenetics is a scientific term and is a relatively new discovery. This seemed to explain why generations of family members fall into the same addiction patterns and problems as one another.

A definition for *epigenetics* that was formulated in 2008 at the Cold Spring Harbor Laboratory in New York is: "an epigenetic trait is a stably heritable phenotype resulting from changes in a chromosome without alterations in the DNA sequence."[1]

Let me break it down. A *phenotype* has the appearance or observation of a genotype; a *genotype* is the sum of genes passed from parent to offspring all packed inside a chromosome; a *chromosome* is a cell that determines our hereditary characteristics, which are passed down through family bloodlines.

So, epigenetics is the study of how behavior and environment can cause changes that affect the way our genes work. Unlike genetic changes, epigenetic changes are reversible and do not change our DNA sequence, but they can change how our body reads a DNA sequence. Diet, obesity, physical activity, smoking, alcohol consumption, psychological stress, or trauma can affect the expression of our genes especially in childhood and even when we are in the womb. Our own genes can convince us of things that are not true and even have the capability to change our original purpose and design. When people are convinced they are "born this way," it's easy to understand and empathize with them, because even though that may be their reality, it was *never* their original design.

I love the fact that epigenetics can be reversed! Change the environment, change the lifestyle, and break the habit! How awesome is that!

Why is this important, you may ask? Well, for two reasons. First, Satan always twists the truth. He damages or tries

to destroy what God has created. For all his efforts, he cannot destroy mankind completely, yet he has used his know-how and understanding of science to distort the human gene code as much as he is able. I love the fact that despite epigenetics being able to affect our genotype, it cannot change the original human DNA code that God created! Remember, Satan cannot create anything; he can only destroy and distort.

Here is a clear explanation on the effect that trauma can have on us in relation to epigenetics.

> A growing body of research suggests that trauma (like from childhood abuse, family violence or food insecurity, among many other things) can be passed from one generation to the next.
>
> …Trauma can leave a chemical mark on a person's genes, which can then be passed down to future generations. This mark doesn't cause a genetic mutation, but it does alter the mechanism by which the gene is expressed.
>
> What would have seemed preposterous 20 years ago has become a fast-emerging field of study. Today the idea that a person's experience could alter their biology, and behavior of their children and grandchildren, has gained serious traction.[2]

When we dedicate our babies in church, we will always pray and break every hereditary curse, disease, sickness, addiction, and lack that has come down through the bloodline in Jesus' Name. It is important we do this because we break off any sins of previous family generations over the baby or child. We are

also breaking negative epigenetics that may have been altered through their genes because of the environment that they have been raised in. Remember, most of us are unaware of how Satan uses science to attack us! When people go through deliverance, breaking generational curses is one of the first things we will do.

An understanding of the whole generational curse traveling down through the bloodline is so important. The word of God speaks in at least three places in the Old Testament about the sins of the fathers being passed down.

> *You shall not bow down to them nor serve them. For I, the Lord your God, am a jealous God, visiting the iniquity of the fathers upon the children to the third and fourth generations of those who hate Me, but showing mercy to thousands, to those who love Me and keep My commandments* (Exodus 20:5-6 NKJV).
>
> *The Lord is longsuffering and abundant in mercy, forgiving iniquity and transgression; but He by no means clears the guilty, visiting the iniquity of the fathers on the children to the third and fourth generation* (Numbers 14:18 NKJV).

It almost seems unfair that God would do this, that children must suffer curses because their parents were wicked, but the children of Israel were not an easy people to parent. With a new understanding of epigenetics (something God has always known), you can understand why God made these statements. Many times, it was because their wickedness against Him was just too much to bear and it increased with every generation. However, God's mercy always outweighed His judgments in

the Old Testament, and we can read in the book of Ezekiel that God refuted His own word.

> *Then another message came to me from the Lord: "Why do you quote this proverb concerning the land of Israel: 'The parents have eaten sour grapes, but their children's mouths pucker at the taste'? As surely as I live, says the Sovereign Lord, you will not quote this proverb anymore in Israel. For all people are mine to judge—both parents and children alike. And this is my rule: The person who sins is the one who will die"* (Ezekiel 18:1-4 NLT).
>
> *"What?" you ask. "Doesn't the child pay for the parent's sins?" No! For if the child does what is just and right and keeps my decrees, that child will surely live. The person who sins is the one who will die. The child will not be punished for the parent's sins, and the parent will not be punished for the child's sins. Righteous people will be rewarded for their own righteous behavior, and wicked people will be punished for their own wickedness* (Ezekiel 18:19-20 NLT).

This here is very important to understand—God Himself no longer punishes generations because of the sins of the fathers. However, epigenetics, curses spoken over family generations, or seeds that Satan has sown still exist, and they still produce and affect our family lines. Ignorance is not an excuse for us. God says in Hosea 4:6, *"My people are destroyed for lack of knowledge."*

As Christians we have access to the greatest revelations, wisdom, and knowledge that we could ever need. A Christian scientist should be the most intellectual, knowledgeable person ever because they are able to tap into the original source of all knowledge—the One who has all the answers to the hows and whys and science of life.

It's encouraging to know that we all stand before God as individuals, and anything that has held us back concerning family history, upbringing, environment, or trauma can be broken off our lives using the most powerful weapon we have as believers—the Name of Jesus! Our childhoods, as traumatic as some of them might have been, should not have the power to hold us back or dictate how we function or how we think. Understanding the ways in which Satan uses our past and the pasts of our parents or family generations to bind and inflict pain and misery on us is the key to breaking the power Satan wields over us. Generational curses can be broken, epigenetics can be changed, and seeds of destruction can be unplucked, dug up, and destroyed!

Notes

1. Shelley L. Berger, et. al, "An operational definition of epigenetics," *Genes and Development*, April 1, 2009, 23(7): 781-783, doi: 10.1101/gad.1787609.
2. Karina Margit Erdelyi, "Can Trauma Be Passed Down From One Generation to the Next?" PStcom.net, August 31, 2022, https://www.psycom.net/trauma/epigenetics-trauma.

CHAPTER 2

IN THE BEGINNING
THE PHONE CALL
THAT STARTED IT ALL

IT WAS A FRIDAY EVENING DURING THE NATIONAL CORONAVI-
rus lockdown. I decided to make a phone call that, unbeknownst
to me, in that one moment would usher in a new season in the
life of our church and my personal ministry. The previous night
we had held a Zoom meeting with the leaders of our church,
and I had noticed that one of our pastors looked as if she was
really struggling. It was a combination of her demeanor and
her lack of interaction in the meeting that caught my attention.

In all fairness, many people's interaction in Zoom meetings
is less than impressive. In fact, I have personally come to dis-
like this type of meeting with a passion. The basic of muting
your mic as essential etiquette seems to escape most people,
and then the lack of thought in device placement is mind-bog-
gling! However, it was quite clear that night that there was
more going on with her than the usual list of misdemeanors.

I knew from a conversation that we had with her husband
the following day that all was not well. He expressed that she
had been feeling quite depressed, that life had gotten on top of

her, and she wasn't coping well with juggling children, ministry, and work. Sadly, the bottom line was that she had become emotionally depleted and had nothing left to give, but up until that night was doing a fairly good job of hiding it from everyone. My first question when I called her didn't come as a surprise to her, and looking back, it was the very question she was desperate for someone to ask. "How are you *really* feeling?"

Almost immediately, she burst into tears, and I, almost like an institutive thing, without thinking in my head, just started quoting every scripture in the word of God that stated how loved she was and how God had a plan for her life. When I ran out of all the scriptures I knew off the top of my head, the Holy Spirit took over! Suddenly, it seemed like I was quoting every scripture from Genesis to Revelation that described her purpose, her calling, her existence, and the love of the Father toward her. Twenty minutes into the phone call of me quoting scripture and speaking in tongues, I could literally sense her shaking on the other end of the phone. Amidst her cries and sobs, she started making a noise that I knew was demonic. At this point I was completely relying on the Holy Spirit and just started to call that demon out in the Name of Jesus. Remembering back, I believe I called out a spirit of depression. With one mighty roar that sounded as if it came from the pit of her stomach, I knew the demon had come out. I was *so* relieved; this was not a normal telephone conversation!

My relief, however, was short-lived! While I was rejoicing that she was free of the demon, almost immediately she said, "There's more." I can clearly remember my thoughts from that night. I was like, "Are you serious?" For the next hour and a half, with the leading of the Holy Spirit, I called out all the demons that had been controlling her thought life and emotional life for years! One by one, and sometimes a couple at a time, they came out. I am unable to recall the number of demons or all their names, but by the end of the phone call she was free and that's all that mattered! I knew she was free when I heard the complete exhaustion in her voice. Suddenly the Holy Spirit filled her with joy, and to hear her laugh from her innermost being was so emotional and a huge relief all at the same time. The biggest plus was that it was the most incredible experience and privilege for me to be on the other end of the phone that night.

I can remember thinking to myself, *What on earth just happened?* I immediately thanked the Lord that He had used me in this way, and I felt extremely humbled for sure! I also felt elation that we had gone into battle with the enemy and had won. I knew this experience was supernatural, yet I could hardly put into words what had just happened. Oh, my goodness, an associate pastor in my church just received deliverance—over the *phone!*

I had a hundred and one questions racing around in my head.

How on earth could my associate pastor be dominated by these demons? We have an awesome church, we worship, we preach the word, we operate in the things of the Holy Spirit! *She* operates in the things of the Holy Spirit!

While I was excited in my spirit for all that had taken place, my mind was questioning the more serious issue of how this happened and how did I not know.

God has the most incredible way of teaching us things when we are not intentionally listening! It benefits us to take note of these lessons; otherwise, we become ignorant of such things and won't see or hear it even if it's right in front of our noses. I was not about to miss this lesson!

All my Christian life I have been aware of the demonic and how demons operate on the earth. I have read books, listened to teaching, and been present in meetings when something "weird" has been going on. In my own life, I have had to deal with them when I have been spiritually attacked, and in all the years we have pastored, we delivered several people. The saddest thing was that the people we delivered were so few that I could remember them all. I recognized that the Holy Spirit was about to teach me something I did not know or had not cared enough to learn about. For years I had been teaching on the last days and that we were in them and what to expect according to prophecy in the word of God, but now the Holy Spirit was going to equip me to live successfully in these days. Deliverance of the saints was going to be a huge part of my ministry.

I was sure my associate pastor would want to keep the whole thing quiet. After all, she had so many people in the church who looked up to her, plus she had been heading up the children's ministry! To my amazement and shock, she made it her mission to share with as many people as would listen. As she expressed to me, she felt that she had literally become born again, again, in that moment. For the first time as a Christian, she felt complete freedom. The weight that had been so heavy for her to carry all those years had been lifted. The feeling she had was incomparable to anything she had ever experienced before. Everything about her changed—the way she looked, the way she spoke. It was as if she was once blind and now she could see! This is the exact experience we are all meant to have when we become born again, yet for her this was the first time she really knew it.

The fruit of her deliverance became more and more evident to us all. (Especially her husband! He was one happy man.) As well as her countenance changing and her spiritual walk being different, everything she put her hand to seemed to prosper! She had her own online business as an artist creating some beautiful, unique paintings. It had been steady yet slow, selling pieces every now and again, but nothing too significant. Within weeks of her deliverance, even her business flourished! Her followers on her social media page tripled overnight, she couldn't get her art out fast enough, it was selling out within minutes of her posting it! It was like she became an overnight success, yet the only difference was that she had been delivered from demons! What blessed me the most in being a spectator of this glorious change in her life was seeing the real person emerge and who she was meant to be all along.

You may ask, "Surely these two things cannot be linked, getting delivered and then your business and finances flourishing?" My answer—a resounding *yes!* Getting delivered changes absolutely everything about you *and* your life! When demons are cast out of you, suddenly you can move, you can see, you can hear and speak with no limitations. When you have demons, they dull your senses; they hinder and affect every area of your life. It's only when you get free of them that you recognize you had not lived in the true freedom the word of God promises to those who become born again. Being a Christian yet not being effective or living your best life is Satan's perfect scenario!

Let me describe it this way, using an example of a kitchen implement—the knife. A knife is a great implement for cutting, slicing and marking; this is what it is made for. However, if the blade of the knife isn't sharp, it stops it from being effective and doing what it was made to do. Many of us have kitchen knives in our drawers that are not as sharp as they used to be; they have lost their original effectiveness, yet most of the time we just leave them sitting there. We sometimes use them for easier jobs that don't require precision cutting or slicing and even sometimes we will use them for jobs they were not made to do. Having a dull blade doesn't stop it from being a knife, but its usefulness diminishes greatly. We don't stop being born again if we have demons, but our ability to do what we are called to do is hindered greatly. We can look the part but have no real effect, and we can even end up doing things that we were never meant to do.

That night truly changed everything! My associate pastor was changed, I was changed, and everyone she met was changed! Without any prayerful planning strategy (we didn't have time!), a new ministry was birthed. In the blink of an eye, I went from delivering someone once a year to several every week! When I look back at how it all started, I am amazed yet not surprised about how God did it. He used one of the least-expected people in our church, a leader, to show people that it's not how long you have been a Christian; it's not about any position you may hold—if demons can find a way into your life, a way they can get in, they will! Demons have no preference when it comes to age, gender, color, or position. If they see an opportunity to enter someone, they won't take a second to think about it.

I know for many Christians who believe that only unsaved people can have demons, this can shake their theology, but as I will explain in other chapters, demons can only attach themselves to the soul part of a human being. To name just one scripture, in James 1:21 (NKJV) our souls are continually being saved by the word of God:

> *Therefore lay aside all filthiness and overflow of wickedness, and receive with meekness the implanted word, which is able to save your souls.*

Demons attach themselves to the soul (mind, will, and emotions) of man and not our spirit. When we become born again, our spirit man, which was dead, in Christ becomes alive, and this is where our communion with the Father, Son, and Holy Spirit takes place. Our spirit man is transformed with the acceptance of who Jesus is and what He has done for us. We are transferred from the kingdom of darkness into the kingdom of light! What was once dead becomes alive! Satan cannot stop you becoming born again. He cannot infiltrate the spirit of a man (unless you are the antichrist!), but he harasses the part of you that must have the word of God to be transformed! Satan fights for the soul of a person to kill, steal, and destroy the very purpose they were made for.

Let me just encourage you though—Jesus commissioned His disciples before He left the earth to cast out demons. We have authority over every demon, principality, and power that attaches itself to us, our church, or our nation. We have the Name of Jesus, the Blood of the Lamb, and the word of God; we have His presence, His power, and His anointing. That

Name which is above every other name commands demons to bow before it,

> *Therefore God also has highly exalted Him and given Him the name which is above every name, that at the name of Jesus every knee should bow, of those in heaven, and of those on earth, and of those under the earth* (Philippians 2:9-10 NKJV).

CHAPTER 3

WHAT, WHEN, AND HOW
OPEN DOORS

DEMONS HAVE PERSONALITIES. THEY ARE WICKED AND EVIL spirits, and depending on the type of demon they are, their character traits will take over a person's personality without them even realizing it! Demons cannot stop the call of God on your life, but they can delay it by making it difficult for you to recognize that God has given you everything needed to accomplish what He has called you to do. Demons will do their best to make you content with living your Christian life without vision, victory, or true freedom in Christ.

While we remember John 10:10 mostly for the second or latter part of the scripture where Jesus declares that He has come to give us life and life more abundantly, the first part of the scripture must be taken seriously and understood. Jesus reminds us that the thief who is Satan comes *only* to kill, steal, and destroy—this is his main objective. If he can't kill you, then he will steal from you, and if that doesn't work, then he will try to destroy you. Maybe he can't take your life, but he will try and make your life a living hell while you're on earth, hoping that you will turn away from God by losing all faith and trust in Him.

Demons will continually make you feel insignificant, not holy enough or good enough. They know pretty much all the Bible, so they will quote scripture to you and use it against you. If you are not aware that demons are on the inside of you and that you are oppressed by them, then you will start to believe *their* thoughts are your thoughts. You will listen unknowingly to what they are saying and start to believe that you are depressed, suicidal, angry, lonely, worried, and full of anxiety. You will start to identify with these traits and believe this is who you are. This is them, not you! The word of God says we have the mind of Christ once we are born again, so every thought that is contrary to God's way of thinking comes from one of two places—our thoughts or a demon's thoughts (masquerading as our thoughts). Satan has the art of suggestion down to a tee; he is a master at this type of attack on the believer, and he uses this strategy repeatedly because it works so well for him. We must not take the thoughts of a demon on, and the way we recognize them is that their thoughts are contrary to what God's word says about us. This is why it says in Romans 12:2 (NKJV) that we are to renew our minds in the word of God:

> *And do not be conformed to this world, but be transformed by the renewing of your mind, that you may prove what is that good and acceptable and perfect will of God.*

Second Corinthians 10:3-6 (NKJV) instructs us to pull down every vain imagination that sets itself up against God's word. In fact, it's one of the clearest scriptures in the Bible that lets us know who we are fighting against—spiritual beings, principalities, powers, rulers of wickedness in heavenly places!

For though we walk in the flesh, we do not war according to the flesh. For the weapons of our warfare are not carnal but mighty in God for pulling down strongholds, casting down arguments and every high thing that exalts itself against the knowledge of God, bringing every thought into captivity to the obedience of Christ, and being ready to punish all disobedience when your obedience is fulfilled.

Before you start panicking, thinking you are demon-possessed or that you somehow have a demon hanging off the back of you, let me say this—*stop, stay calm,* and carry on! I am going to break it all down for you in the next couple of chapters. Trust me, there will be no gray areas left untouched. You will *know* by the end of this whether you need deliverance (welcome to the club!), and you will understand the significance of the deliverance ministry for the church in these last days. Then, most importantly, you will know how you can personally operate in deliverance, bringing hope and freedom to others.

First, let me explain to you *how* and *when* demons gain entry and then answer the question of exactly *where* they enter in the next chapter.

Trauma of any kind is usually the open door that initially allows a demon to enter. Once they are in, they will wait for opportune moments to start to distort how you think and feel about yourself, and because there is no time frame with them, this could happen straightaway or years after you have experienced that initial trauma. Whatever area you have experienced trauma in—sexual, emotional, or physical—is the point where the distortion will start. Demons will do this through your mind and your thought processes, which will then affect your will and emotions, ultimately heading for your heart, as you will read in the next chapter.

As in the case of my associate pastor, it was her past that had opened a door in her life when she was a little girl, illustrating my earlier point that messed-up adults are generally a result of messed-up childhoods. Every experience in our lives creates good or bad memories that stay with us right through to the day we die. Not all memories are significant or bad, which is why we forget some things, although a song or a smell will remind us of our past as if it happened only yesterday. The problem is the memories that *are* bad—the ones we have fought hard to forget, the ones we have put to the very back of our minds, wishing or pretending they never happened. We know if we think about them, they will take us to a dark place in our minds and even cause our bodies to physically react. The moment we think of them, it's like being transported back in time. We feel bound and restricted with fear, guilt, shame, or terror. It's these types of feelings that allow demons to enter. The trauma attracts them, and our emotions open a spiritual door into our soul (mind, will, and emotions), and whether it's in our past or something we are experiencing now, it's what allows a demon to gain access.

Let me clarify. Demons gain their entry in our lives through traumatic experiences that produce, to name a few, fear, guilt, shame, violence, rejection, abandonment, or terror. These come through sin, which we have committed in our past or present, but also, sadly, often it is through sin that has been committed *against* us. The experiences are as individual as we are, and here

are just a few examples of open doors or entry points where demons have come in. Hopefully knowing this will help you gain a clearer understanding of demonic oppression and bring clarity to how demons operate.

Entrance Through Abuse

This would be the longest book ever written if I wrote down an account of every person I have delivered as a direct result of abuse. Abuse comes in various forms—physical, sexual, and emotional. It could be any one or all three of these abuses that has happened to you, or you may have been witness to the abuse of a family member or friend, or you could be the perpetrator of the abuse. Whatever category you fit into, demons don't care—they just see an open door and they take their opportunity. Abuse is a violation against us; it doesn't seek permission, it just demands our compliance. Abuse will take something that doesn't belong to it, leaving the abused person feeling robbed and defiled. This is the very nature of a demon; they steal what doesn't belong to them. Demons of abuse will make their hosts feel guilty and shamed for being abused and will try and make them hate themselves for something that was completely out of their control. Recovery without deliverance is possible, but the feelings, consequences, or resulting behavior of that abuse will often remain. Deliverance gets rid of all of it because it casts out the demons that are inflicting the pain in the first place.

One of the first people I remember delivering was a 40-year-old lady who had been sexually abused by her father when she was a little girl. He would have her sit on his lap and proceed to grope her body parts. While he never had sexual intercourse

with her, he would grope her on a regular basis; it also extended to a relative of hers. Neither girl spoke about it because of shame and, in a weird kind of way, to protect her father. For years she buried it, but all through her teenage years she suffered confusion about her sexuality and as a result hated the way she looked.

When she received deliverance, some of the demonic spirits that had entered her were fear, shame, guilt, abuse, sexual perversion, sadness, low self-esteem, lesbianism, and confusion. All these demons were able to gain entry or attachment initially through the spirit or demon of fear. The trauma of abuse by someone who should have been her protector caused her emotions of fear and guilt to overwhelm her.

When you have experienced abuse, whoever is the perpetrator, it alters the way you see yourself, what you believe you are worth, what you believe you deserve or don't deserve. It can even alter your sexuality. The confusion a spirit of abuse brings can completely change the trajectory of a person's life. It's that brain-altering condition called epigenetics where the phenotype (if you remember) is a genotype that has been altered because of environment, surroundings, or experience. Epigenetic traits are really common in people who have suffered abuse. Listen to this startling explanation of the damage it can cause in a young person:

> Young brains are particularly sensitive to epigenetic changes. Experiences very early in life, when the brain is developing most rapidly, cause epigenetic adaptations that influence whether, when, and how genes release their instructions

for building future capacity for health, skills, and resilience.[1]

When a young life has been traumatized, their personality and their God-given purpose has already started to change. In my experience, abuse is the most powerful change agent of the emotions in someone's life. It changes them from what they were purposed to be in their life to something dictated to by an unseen attack from the enemy. That lively child, the bubbly young girl, the person who was the life and soul of the party, the one who would never stop talking—it is all affected by the demonic spirit of abuse.

When it's sexual abuse that occurs at a young age, it can affect the person so much that they lose all sense of what is right and what is wrong as they grow up. They struggle to see themselves as God created them. As well as changing their personality, as I've already stated, it can also change and alter their sexual orientation. This is because sexual abuse is a perversion of what God originally created sex for. It's that knowing of what is right and what is wrong that gets clouded and confused. A sexually abused person just wants to feel secure and loved no matter where that love or affirmation is coming from.

The good news in all of this is that even if you have suffered abuse of any kind, it doesn't have to be a permanent change— deliverance can set the captive free! The blood of Jesus, the word of God, and the casting out of demons can reverse any damage that has been caused through physical, sexual, or emotional abuse. It's only God who can make a person feel clean, pure, and brand-new from the inside out!

Entrance Through Abandonment and Rejection

This is one of the most interesting routes that can lead to demonic oppression. Not always, but most times people who have been abandoned when they were young—maybe left by their parents, given up for adoption, or not wanted in the womb—are directly harassed by demons. Demons can gain entrance primarily through rejection by a parent. However, rejection can also come from a spouse, a partner, or even a schoolteacher, and it is a spirit of rejection that will enter a person. The door opens because of what has been continually spoken about the individual by someone who has authority over them. The reason this is interesting is because when the feeling of being left, abandoned, or rejected comes and the demon enters, it also brings along with it a spirit of rebellion and anger.

I remember delivering a young girl of about ten years of age. Her mother was at her wits' end with her. She was unruly, angry, disobedient, and would continually lie and make up outrageous stories to gain attention for herself and get people into trouble. When we delved into her history, we discovered that while the mum was eight months pregnant with her, the father beat the mum severely. Not only did he attack the mum, but he also repeatedly screamed that he didn't want the baby she was carrying and tried to kill the baby in her womb by strangling the mum. Thankfully, he was not successful, but the demons were able to gain entry because of the power of a parent's actions and words over their unborn child.

The spirit of rejection had gained access in the womb. Then, when she was born, it opened the door to many other spirits as she grew up. Spirits of rebellion, violence, aggression, lying,

and the spirit of feeling unloved. The mum could not understand why the daughter displayed these traits as she was no longer with the father and, as much as she was able, showed love and kindness toward her daughter. The problem was that the demons had already gained entrance. When she was born, the child was already demonized. Her mother explained that she had always been a difficult child, and even as a baby she was continually agitated and would hardly ever settle. It was not surprising—those demons had already taken over the girl's personality, and being a young child, she had very little defense against such demons. Until we cast them out, the spirits of rejection and everything else that had entered were able to influence the soul of the daughter, causing bad behavior even from babyhood.

People who suffer with these types of demons from a very young age, because they have grown up with them, have very little awareness that this is the problem and will just assume, "This is the way I am." Sadly, parents who have no idea that this is the problem will take their children to the doctors and have them treated medically to try to cure, calm, or control the symptoms they are displaying.

There seems to be a diagnosis for every bad behavioral trait, and Satan loves that our children are being medicated at a faster speed than sound! Have you noticed the increase in diagnoses of ADHD, Asperger's syndrome, and autism over the last ten years?

Please hear me—I'm not saying that all children affected by these medical diagnoses or who have these symptoms have been demonized. But there are many for whom the root cause is not

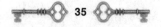

a deficit in their learning capacity, but it really is a demon. We can't imagine this is possible, especially that this could happen to an innocent baby, but that's when demons take their opportunity—at the most vulnerable time of our lives. Where is more vulnerable than when we are in our mother's womb?

I mentioned adoption and want to address this with as much sensitivity as possible. A spirit of rejection along with rebellion will always try and gain entrance to a baby or child who has been adopted. If you have adopted or fostered children, you may understand what I am saying. Maybe you have been adopted yourself, and as much as you have received love and care from the parents who raised you, there is still that emotion of rejection that rears its ugly head every now and again. The feeling of needing to be the best and impress those around you never goes away; the need to prove that you deserve what you have is endless, yet the underlying feelings of abandonment never quite go away. Anger is sometimes bubbling under the surface because of the situation you find yourself in, which was nothing to do with you.

I find it so interesting that people who have been adopted from the youngest age, even two weeks old, will still struggle with their identity and ultimately end up struggling with the feelings of rejection. We have prayed for many people in this situation. They will always say that they have so much love for the parents that raised them, but they still can't shake the deep-seated feeling of not being good enough. It's amazing to see, when that spirit of rejection is cast out of them, and the transformation begins to take place, they receive freedom and gain confidence in their identity because of the overwhelming sense

of Jesus' love for them. Praise God that the spirits of abandonment, rebellion, and anger must leave along with the spirit of rejection in the Name of Jesus!

Entrance Through Pornography

Pornography is one of the biggest entry doors in the lives of humans. It may not always be through a bad experience that you encountered pornography; it could be because you have stumbled upon it at some point in your life. I will say, however, that most people who have been sexually abused or have had sexual experiences at a young age will have an addiction to pornography. The spirit of pornography will enter and take a hold of you if you become addicted to it, and all your willpower in the world will not be able to break you free from it.

The origins of this perversion originally started with Satan and his fallen angels perverting the beautiful gift of intimacy between a man and a woman. Nowhere more clearly can we see this than in Genesis 17 when we read the account of Sodom and Gomorrah and the sexual perversion that was taking place in that city. However, even further back in Genesis 6, we can read about the sons of God knowing or taking the daughters of men. The act of "knowing" one wife or one husband exclusively was a gift given from God to man. It meant forsaking all others for the purpose of creating new life on earth. Adam knew Eve, Abraham knew Sarah, and so on and so forth, but these heavenly beings stepped outside of their domain and had relations with human women. This was an abomination before God.

From the beginning we can see how Satan perverted sex. Sexual intercourse was created exclusively between a male and female, but both in Genesis 6 and 17 we find it had been perverted by the sons of God, the heavenly beings, with the daughters of men—human women who were willingly having sex with them, which produced the Nephilim, the race of giants. Its why God made the statement in Genesis 6:5-6 (NLT):

> *The Lord observed the extent of human wicked-*
> *ness on the earth, and he saw that everything they*
> *thought or imagined was consistently and totally*
> *evil. So the Lord was sorry he had ever made them*
> *and put them on the earth. It broke his heart.*

Pornography became another distortion of God's creation of sex, and Satan realized he could snare billions of people with this kind of perversion.

Pornography is a huge lie. It takes what God has created, which is the act and enjoyment of sex between one man and one woman within the boundaries and security of marriage, and completely distorts its enjoyment and purpose. Instead of looking to your spouse to satisfy you—their body, their personality, their love for you—pornography leads us to believe that sex can be enjoyed just as much if not more as a selfish act on your own or with a stranger who doesn't require anything from you. The only demand that pornography has is self-gratification. Sex within marriage is all about loving and satisfying the other person and forsaking all others. Pornography is a selfish act all about satisfying self.

If Satan can blind us into thinking pornography is just another form of sex, then his plan to pollute our minds and hearts with perverted and distorted images of one another has no end. He can continually add definitions of what sex is while all along perverting the purity of what God originally created sex for. Today's distorted understanding of sex has produced a culture where any sexual act is becoming permissible.

Even though the world believes the lie that pornography is an alternative way of having sex, most believers have an overwhelming feeling of guilt once they have participated in it. Your conscience feels scarred, and your heart confirms that it's just not right. Yes, you read correctly—I said when *believers* participate in it! Studies show that over 50 percent of Christians, including pastors and leaders, admit to practicing pornography on a regular basis!

Demons gain entrance through pornography because it's sin. It's a hidden sin that no one else knows about. It's done in private, and once you have tried it, it can become addictive very quickly. Once you become addicted, demons enter. The thing with demons is they are perverted, unclean, and will twist everything.

Not everyone, but many people go from watching straight sex to homosexual sex to multiple people engaging in sex. For a minority of people, the demons twist things even further and they end up watching sex with young children and even sex with animals. This is one of Satan's greatest weapons against humanity. The demons involved are some of the worst, most twisted, dark, and devious demons we encounter. Pornography not only perverts our minds, but it also condemns our heart

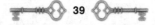

because we sin against ourselves. It's hidden, it causes anxiety, it brings confusion, it leaves a person unable to be satisfied with God's gift of intimacy and sex with their spouse, it distorts our view of the opposite sex, and it leaves us empty and void of satisfaction. It's the great deception that promises to make us feel complete yet does the exact opposite and, in fact, leaves us feeling dirty, guilty, and ashamed.

Because pornography is readily available to us 24/7, mainly via our mobile phones, it's one of the easiest sins to get addicted to and one of the most difficult to break free from. Most people have encountered pornography at some time in their life, and for those who encountered it when they were young, it seems an addiction to it is inevitable. I wouldn't be exaggerating if I said ninety percent of those we deliver have an issue with pornography, both men and women, with most starting at a young age. It may not even be the main reason they come for deliverance, but it seems to always be there somewhere in the background. It really is a difficult addiction to break, and even when people have been delivered from it, they must work hard at keeping free by not entertaining anything that could lead them back into it.

With any kind of deliverance, we will always encourage people to get rid of anything connected or associated with what they've been delivered from. With pornography, we encourage people to avoid watching or listening to anything with sexual content in it, especially when they are alone. We advise them not to spend ages in the bath or shower or even extended time in bed! I know this may sound extreme, but it works! You must replace those moments with spending time worshiping and praying. Deliverance gets rid of the demons, but it's the responsibility of the person to keep themselves free from any entering back in.

Entrance Through Addiction

Addiction causes us to be out of control. We cannot control it; it controls us! In the book of Genesis, God specifically instructs man to have dominion and authority over the earth and everything that He has created in the earth.

> *Then God said, "Let Us make man in Our image, according to Our likeness; let them have dominion over the fish of the sea, over the birds of the air, and over the cattle, over all the earth and over every creeping thing that creeps on the earth"* (Genesis 1:26 NKJV).

According to the dictionary, *dominion* means "the power or right of governing and controlling, sovereign authority." We are meant to have power over everything on this earth. It's not something we attain to; it is something we have that was given to us originally by God, lost by Adam, but then regained by Jesus when He conquered all the powers of darkness on the cross. The dictionary definition of *addiction* is "a state of being compulsively committed to a habit or practice or to something that is psychologically or physically habit-forming, as drugs, to such an extent that its cessation causes severe trauma." Suddenly the substance, the alcohol, the porn, the drugs or whatever else we are addicted to has dominion over us, which is the opposite of how we should be living. It's a distortion of what God intended

for man—that we should be in control and have dominion over things instead of things having dominion and control over us. Satan turns the tables in his favor.

Demons take advantage of this and once they are in, it is almost impossible to kick the addiction out through natural processes. Am I saying charities and organizations set up to help people overcome addictions don't work? Not at all; of course they work, *but* they cannot free someone completely of that addiction. Most ex-addicts work exceptionally hard to avoid "falling off the wagon" or going back into the addiction they have struggled with. If you've had any experience in this area, either as an ex-addict or someone helping an addict, you will know that the journey is relentless. It must be hard fought and without compromise.

It is one of the hardest roads to travel with a Christian because the very nature of addiction causes the person to be dependent on the addiction rather than on God. That is why they need deliverance, because it removes the problem at its root—the problem being the demons. It's almost irrelevant what the addiction is. It's the same wicked demon that has entered a person. It then allows the demons of the thing to which the person is addicted to enter, such as a spirit of pornography, obesity, alcohol, gambling, etc. Another reason the route of counseling or therapy to cure addictions can't work solely on its own is because a spiritual door has been opened and nothing in the natural world can overcome demons in the spiritual world. Determination, a strong self-will, goals, or classes cannot have dominion over the kingdom of darkness. It is only authority used in the Name of Jesus that demons respond to and are subject to.

Addictions can come in the form of alcohol, pornography, drugs, obesity, OCD, caffeine, gambling, and anything else that you cannot control in the natural. It goes beyond self-control and "trying" to be good. You can identify if you have a spirit of addiction in your life by not being able to live or function without the thing that you are addicted to. Just like the dictionary definition says, you have no control over it. When a spirit of addiction has entered, it must be cast out first before the spirits of the things you are addicted to can be broken and cast out. If this doesn't happen, the addiction will remain and all the feelings of needing the "fix" will come back later.

Before we were confident in operating fully in the ministry of deliverance, we would pray repeatedly for people struggling with all kinds of addictions. Demons would leave when they were cast out, but because we didn't cast out the strongman of addiction, it would allow all the ones we had cast out to come back again the moment the person had a weak moment. The individuals would be fine for a while, but then be drawn back into whatever they were addicted to. It was hard to watch because the feeling of failure would be overwhelming for both them and us. As we grew in this ministry, the Holy Spirit revealed to us *how* we should cast this demon out and then how we should deal with the rest.

As I explain in later chapters, the ministry of deliverance is not just one quick prayer. Deliverance is a process. Time is taken to talk through a person's past, bringing to light buried and hidden things. Addictions of all kinds are always the result of some other trauma that has taken place in a person's life, and talking is the way we get to the root of it.

Entrance Through Sin

Most demons have gained entrance to us before we are born again, but demons still have access to us as believers if we are in sin. If we continue to sin in areas we have been forgiven for, the door will remain open, so even though your spirit man is born again and you can have communion and fellowship with the Father, Son, and Holy Spirit, you are still choosing to allow Satan access to your soul man through continuing to sin. The Christian walk is one of dying to the flesh and walking in the spirit. Sin is making a conscious choice to walk in the flesh, and if we do this, we will never fulfill all that God has called us to do or ever be free of demonic influence or oppression. It never ceases to amaze me how many Christians still live like they are in the world. They have a relationship with the Lord, they are filled with the Holy Spirit, yet they still practice sin and think it's acceptable because they don't see any physical consequences.

I am truly not a "holier than thou" believer, but honestly some of the excuses Christians give for practicing sin are shocking! Let me just make things plain and clear and give you a list of the following sins that will allow demons to enter you as a Christian if you choose to practice sin: sex outside of marriage, addiction to pornography, masturbation, continually drinking alcohol and getting drunk, dishonesty, lying, abusive behavior toward people, always being angry at someone or something.

Sin could also take the form of unforgiveness or offense. The word of God is clear when it comes to unforgiveness. We are told in Matthew 6:14-15 (NKJV):

> *For if you forgive men their trespasses, your heavenly Father will also forgive you. But if you do not forgive men their trespasses, neither will your Father forgive your trespasses.*

When we stand praying and asking God for anything, we must forgive our brother first; otherwise, God will not and cannot answer our prayers.

> *And whenever you stand praying, if you have anything against anyone, forgive him, that your Father in heaven may also forgive you your trespasses. But if you do not forgive, neither will your Father in heaven forgive your trespasses* (Mark 11:25-26 NKJV).

When we become offended by a family member, a church leader, a brother or a sister in the church, or a work colleague, and we choose to live in offense, then demons will come in like a flood, and with one will come many! This sin is a favorite of theirs—they love to control believers within the church. In fact, that's where they can be most effective and cause the greatest damage. Demons love it when believers get offended and start to live with unforgiveness in their heart. Demons know what God's word says and so they know that believers will struggle to get their prayers answered if they don't forgive as God has instructed them to. They then influence believers and convince them that God's word isn't completely true because He's not

answering their prayers! Again, I need to say that neither Satan nor his demons can stop us becoming born again, but they can stop or delay us in fulfilling God's call on our lives.

When demons are present in believers, poverty, failure, confusion, instability, low self-esteem, apathy, division, accusation, witchcraft, a religious spirit, to name just a few, will show up in the church.

I know it's a lot to take in, especially as these entrances or open doors I've described are just a few areas where this can happen. Please be encouraged though, as you have read this chapter and as you continue to read through the book, just know the enemy *is* defeated. Jesus said He came to expose and destroy the works of darkness, and our job is to carry out His instructions in full.

> *For this purpose the Son of God was manifested, that He might destroy the works of the devil* (1 John 3:8 NKJV).
>
> *Having disarmed principalities and powers, He made a public spectacle of them, triumphing over them in it* (Colossians 2:15).

Note

1. "Epigenetics and Child Development: How Children's Experiences Affect Their Genes," Harvard, https://developingchild.harvard.edu/resources/what-is-epigenetics-and-how-does-it-relate-to-child-development.

CHAPTER 4

WHERE DEMONS ENTER
IT'S A HEART ISSUE

THIS IS AN IMPORTANT CHAPTER, AND HOPEFULLY IT WILL make everything else make sense. To fully understand, we need to go right back to the beginning—to the book of Genesis, when Adam and Eve sinned and were cut off from the source of all life and impartation.

> Then the Lord God said, "Behold, the man has become like one of Us, to know good and evil. And now, lest he put out his hand and take also of the tree of life, and eat, and live forever"—therefore the Lord God sent him out of the garden of Eden to till the ground from which he was taken. So, He drove out the man; and He placed cherubim at the east of the garden of Eden, and a flaming sword which turned every way, to guard the way to the tree of life (Genesis 3:22-24 NKJV).

On the day Adam and Eve sinned, they died spiritually, emotionally, and physically! In an instant, their relationship with God, with one another, and with the whole of creation changed. They died spiritually because their spirit man was disconnected from God because of the sin of disobedience they had committed. The glory and the fellowship they once enjoyed with God abruptly ended. They died emotionally because everything that was familiar to them—all that they knew, their confidence in who they were, and their surroundings—changed in an instant. They died physically because no longer would they live forever. Decay, sin, and death would affect their bodies and minds in ways they could never have imagined.

Why was it such a dramatic shift? It was their heart attitude toward God that caused this sudden turn of events. Eve had heard something new about God which she believed, pondered in her heart, and then shared her thoughts with Adam. The moment they both believed in their hearts that God was keeping something from them was the moment they spiritually disconnected from Him and took on the nature of the father of lies, Satan himself. They were still full of knowledge and full of understanding, but now it would be with a wicked and evil intent of the heart! They believed in their hearts what Satan had said, and the fruit of that belief was seen through their actions when they hid from God.

> *And they heard the sound of the Lord God walking in the garden in the cool of the day, and Adam and his wife hid themselves from the presence of the Lord God among the trees of the garden. Then the Lord God called to Adam and said to him, "Where are you?" So he said, "I heard Your voice in the garden, and I was afraid because I was naked; and I hid myself." And He said, "Who told you that you were naked? Have you eaten form the tree of which I*

commanded you that you should not eat?" (Genesis 3:8-11 NKJV).

Satan took this opportune moment with both hands to steal God's creation from Him. Adam and Eve's death in all its forms would be seen throughout the ages and centuries, affecting all generations, families, and bloodlines. They went from being connected to God (the source of continued life) to being connected with Satan (the source of all wickedness and death), and it was their newfound belief in their heart that connected them!

Of course, we can take great comfort that God, our heavenly Father, had a plan of rescue for His creation. He was not about to leave us to become the full embodiment of Satan. Left with no hope, that's what would have happened.

God wasn't taken by surprise, however, and addressed Satan about his future.

> *And I will put enmity between you and the woman, and between your seed and her Seed; He shall bruise your head, and you shall bruise His heel* (Genesis 3:15 NKJV).

The New American Standard Bible replaces the word *Seed* with *Descendant*. We know God is referring to His Son Jesus and that Jesus would be born through a woman. Her Seed would ultimately defeat Satan, reversing the effects of all that had taken place in the Garden. God had already made a way, but it would require a new decision to be made by man.

God knew that the issue lay with the heart of man and that through sin it had become evil and only a new heart would fully reverse the process of death and sever us from Satan and his control over us. The *only* way the removal of sin could be done would be by sending His Son to die on the cross for humanity. Only by receiving His Son, Jesus Christ, into our hearts, the place that death had infiltrated, could we be redeemed in our heart from the curse of death.

We must understand that the original sin was birthed in the heart! It's the same place it started for Satan when he was in heaven, and this is where it started with Eve in the garden. The thought may have been put in her mind initially by Satan, but the decision to take the fruit and eat of it was made in her heart!

> *The heart is deceitful above all things, and desperately wicked; who can know it? I, the Lord, search the heart, I test the mind, even to give every man according to his ways, according to the fruit of his doings* (Jeremiah 17:9-10 NKJV).

We know God's word says that all of life's issues flow from the heart, so it's vitally important that we pay attention to the state of our heart, what we believe, and who has ownership over it! I have listed four different translations of the same scripture for the purpose of gaining understanding of how important it is to protect our hearts. The key words in each scripture all have the same significance, essence, and connotation—keep, watch, guard *above all else*—which suggests that taking care of our heart *is* the most important thing.

> *Keep your heart with all diligence, for out of it spring the issues of life* (Proverbs 4:23).
> *Watch over your heart with all diligence, for from it flow the springs of life* (Proverbs 4:23 NASB).

Guard your heart above all else, for it is the source of life (Proverbs 4:23 CSB).

Above all else, guard your heart, for everything you do flows from it (Proverbs 4:23 NIV).

It's also important to remember this fact—the only power Satan has over us is the suggestions and accusations targeted at our mind. He knows that thoughts meditated and reasoned over long enough will go down into our heart, and once they are in our heart, those thoughts start to become truth to us. This is what he did with Eve. He suggested a different view by accusing God of withholding good things from them. She thought about it, then believed it, then spoke it out to Adam. Both our spirit man and our soul man are connected by our heart. What we believe in our heart will dictate how we speak and how we live our lives!

I pray that the eyes of your heart may be enlightened, so that you will know what is the hope of His calling (Ephesians 1:18 NASB).

For the word of God is living and active and sharper than any two-edged sword, and piercing as far as the division of soul and spirit, of both joints and marrow, and able to judge the thoughts and intentions of the heart (Hebrews 4:12 NASB).

It's amazing that it's our heart that gets the final say over everything and that our hearts have the capacity to see, think, and listen! Having been made in the image of God, in His likeness, man has the appearance of God and the ability to be like Him if we receive Jesus Christ into our heart as our Lord and

Savior. If we do this, the life flow is reconnected, the relationship is restored, and our spirit man is alive once again.

We are a three-part being—body, soul, and spirit:

> *Now may the God of peace Himself sanctify you completely; and may your whole spirit, soul, and body be preserved blameless at the coming of our Lord Jesus Christ* (1 Thessalonians 5:23 NKJV).

The most common way to describe man is that we are a spirit being, we have a soul, and we live in a body, but our heart is a separate entity. The heart is the connecter between our soul and spirit. The heart is what governs our belief system, and we are either ruled by our soul man (flesh) or our spirit man. The heart will believe whatever it learns from either one or both. Unless you are born again, however, your spirit man is dead, or disconnected from God, which is why Satan and his demons can influence unbelievers easily because they are governed completely by their flesh or soul part. Our spirit only comes alive or reconnects with God when we believe in our heart and confess with our mouth that Jesus Christ is Lord.

> *That if you confess with your mouth the Lord Jesus and believe in your heart that God has raised Him from the dead, you will be saved. For with the heart one believes unto righteousness, and with the mouth confession is made unto salvation* (Romans 10:9-10 NKJV).

This is why Satan targeted and questioned Eve's belief system in the garden. He knew if she believed him, the result

would be catastrophic! His intent was to separate and manipulate Eve all along.

The heart will always be full of whatever we have been meditating on or allowing ourselves to watch or hear via our spirit or soul man. Again, our heart determines our belief system—what we truly believe without having to think about it—and once we believe something in our heart, it's very difficult to think otherwise. It's like we bypass our thought system because we just know that we know certain things. For example, on a positive note, I know my Savior is Jesus Christ; I don't have to think about it because He is in my heart; it's what I both know and believe. I know that I love my husband; it's not something I have to think about or make myself feel it; I just know it. My belief system is that I have a Savior whom I love, and I have a husband whom I love; nobody can convince me otherwise because it's settled in my heart.

Demons cannot gain access directly to your heart or to your spirit man, but they can invade your soul man. If your soul man is full of their influence, then it will influence your heart. Are you still with me? Okay, this is so important to understand and exactly what God's word tells us to do—we *must* guard our heart above *all* things. The word in Proverbs 4:23 is so clear to us that whatever is *in* our heart will flow *out* of our mouth. Remember, what was in Eve's heart came out of her mouth when she spoke those words to Adam! The scripture says, "*Keep your heart with all diligence, for out of it spring the issues of life.*" I also love the New Living Translation of this verse: "*Guard your heart above all else, for it determines the course of your life.*"

If the influence of demonic behavior is ruling our mind, will, and emotions (soul man) then our heart, which is our belief system, will lean on the side of believing what they are saying to us. We will start to see ourselves that way and act accordingly. Demons will convince you it is the real you! You can still be a Christian, but any breakthrough or victory will seem impossible. You will be swayed when it comes to the word of God. Satan hates a believer knowing or practicing God's word, so if he can influence hearts through the soul of a man not to believe God, then he can quite easily control a Christian.

Our soul, which again is made up of our mind, will and emotions, also makes up our personality. This is something else important to understand. We recognize a person by how they look on the outside, but we really *see* and know a person by what's on the inside. Most of us would describe a person briefly by their outward appearance but mostly by their personality. For instance, if I was describing my husband, I would refer to his appearance briefly but then would say he's a lovely guy, always happy, a real bubbly personality. I identify the real him by what is on the inside of him.

The behavior that we display on the outside is generally the reflection of what is on the inside. Demons will try to replace our personalities with theirs, using our mind, will, and emotions to convince us that the feelings of insecurity, depression, weakness, jealousy, anger (the list is endless) are part of our personality type and who we are. Satan knows it's the inside of us that is the real person, and that the inside dictates what we do on the outside. This is why we are implored to guard out heart. We must recognize and know who the real "us" is so that our belief on the inside lines us up with God's word and what *He* says about us. Demons cause all sorts of confusion to those they have entered, to the point that even though we are believers, we can lose ourselves among all the emotions that we feel. If you have been demonized in later life, you will miss the person you used to be! You will feel desperate to get back to the real you, but this can only happen if the demons are cast out of you along with their personalities that have been dominating you.

Satan is out to kill, steal, and destroy us, and his target is our heart! If he can penetrate our heart with his lies and deception, then he can change everything we are and believe, and our behavior will become the reflection of what we feel on the inside.

Satan's ultimate target is the heart of man, and he will use us to defeat us, if that makes sense. If he can infiltrate man's heart, he can say and do anything to turn man not only against his creator God but also against himself. He can separate him from the One who loves him the most. The soul of man is the most vulnerable place because it's man that must keep it in check. It's our responsibility to continually renew our mind in the word of God. It's our responsibility to allow the word of God to clean us up and change the way we think, act, and speak from the inside out. It comes down to *us,* and because of this Satan knows we are an easy target! His attack against humanity and the way he does it is the same as in the garden in the beginning. However, I love the fact that God's plan of redemption for mankind involved all who were present in the beginning—Himself, the Son, and Holy Spirit! God knew how difficult it would be for us to overcome the enemy, which is why after Jesus' death, burial, and resurrection, He gave us His Holy Spirit to help us.

> *I will pray the Father, and He will give you another*
> *Helper, that He may abide with you forever—the*

Spirit of truth, whom the world cannot receive, because it neither sees Him nor knows Him: but you know Him, for He dwells with you and will be in you. I will not leave you orphans; I will come to you (John 14:16-18 NKJV).

The Holy Spirit fills us, guides us, and empowers us, and we cannot live this life without Him. I want to encourage you to keep building a strong, dependent relationship with Him so that you can live a successful Christian life—body, soul, and spirit.

So, let's recap. Having read the previous chapter along with this chapter, we can conclude that demons gain entrance into our lives through traumatic experiences in our past and sometimes in our present. I have covered it previously; we also know that demons can enter us and attach themselves to us through family generations. The doorway is through our soul, which is our mind, our will, and our emotions. Once they are in or attached to us, they convince us that their personality of anger, fear, hatred, low self-esteem, etc. is our personality. If we think this way, eventually our heart will start to believe this, and we will begin to live the kind of life dictated to us by these emotions. We are still able to function and call ourselves a Christian, but we are not living in complete freedom. We will always struggle to hear God's voice or see the path He has planned for us. It's essential, therefore, as a believer that we recognize why our minds and our hearts are to be fiercely guarded at all costs!

CHAPTER 5

BUT I'M A CHRISTIAN
CAN CHRISTIANS HAVE DEMONS?

Now may the God of peace Himself sanctify you completely; and may your whole spirit, soul, and body be preserved blameless at the coming of our Lord Jesus Christ. He who calls you is faithful, who also will do it.
—1 THESSALONIANS 5:23-24 NKJV

Therefore lay aside all filthiness and overflow of wickedness, and receive with meekness the implanted word, which is able to save your souls.
—JAMES 1:21 NKJV

I WANT TO DEBUNK THE BIGGEST MYTH IN THE MODERN-DAY church that Christians cannot have demons! If this is true, then I'm not sure who I've been casting demons out of all this time! If you have reached this point in the book, then already you will have read testimonies of Christians being set free through deliverance! As we have already covered in a previous chapter, demons inhabit the soul part of a person and not the spirit of a

person, and this is the revelation that gives us the understanding that yes, indeed, Christians can have demons. When we become born again, the supernatural transference takes place in our spirit man, not the soul man. Our spirit, which was once dead because of sin, is now alive. The spirit of a person wakes up when they believe by faith in their heart that Christ died and rose from the dead for them.

> *For with the heart one believes unto righteousness, and with the mouth confession is made unto salvation* (Romans 10:10 NKJV).

It's our spirit man that wakes up when we believe:

> *It is the spirit that quickeneth; the flesh profiteth nothing: the words that I speak unto you, they are spirit, and they are life* (John 6:63 KJV).

The supernatural part of our relationship with God is restored and the communication lines are now open.

Remember Nicodemus, the leader of the Jews in John 3 and the conversation he and Jesus had in the garden at night. Nicodemus wanted to know who Jesus really was because he knew that somehow He had come from God because of all the signs He was able to perform. Jesus made the statement in John 3:3 (NKJV):

> *Jesus answered and said to him, "Most assuredly, I say to you, unless one is born again, he cannot see the kingdom of God."*

Immediately Nicodemus' response was, "How could one be born again? How could you go back into your mother's womb?" Of course, we know that Jesus was referring to a spiritual birth;

we are so familiar with this term *born again*, but back then no one had heard of anything like this. Jesus made it clear that this had to happen in order to have a relationship with the Father and enter the kingdom of God.

> *Jesus answered, "Most assuredly, I say to you, unless one is born of water and the Spirit, he cannot enter the kingdom of God. That which is born of the flesh is flesh, and that which is born of the Spirit is spirit"* (John 3:5-6 NKJV).

The soul part of man, which is made up of our mind, will and emotions, technically hasn't changed, and so from the moment of salvation it embarks on a journey of being saved or renewed by the word of God. It is not a quick fix overnight! In an instant we are saved; our spirit man on the inside of us is made alive in Christ, and by receiving Jesus in our hearts as our Lord and Savior we are transferred out of the kingdom of darkness into the kingdom of light. The salvation, or should I say the transformation, of our soul man then begins to take place when we renew our mind in the word of God, and when the word becomes engrafted into our hearts. The word tells us in Philippians 2:12 that we continually work out our salvation with fear and trembling, which means it is a process for our souls to be saved. So, the miracle of salvation takes place in the spirit of a person in an instant, but the natural part of a man or woman begins the journey of transformation!

> *For He has rescued us from the kingdom of darkness and transferred us into the Kingdom of his dear Son, who purchased our freedom and forgave our sins* (Colossians 1:13-14 NLT).

When we are born again, saved, and redeemed, we are born of the Spirit of God and then instructed to be baptized in water to signify the old man dying, cut off from the way we used to do things. It's an outward demonstration or testimony of an inward act or transformation that has taken place. The old man or life is buried, and the new life, born of the Spirit of God, rises up out of the water. We are then baptized in the Holy Spirit. It's the infilling of the power of God. Jesus specifically told His disciples to wait to evangelize until they received the power they needed to do it effectively:

> And being assembled together with them, He commanded them not to depart from Jerusalem, but to wait for the Promise of the Father, "which," He said, "you have heard from Me; for John truly baptized with water, but you shall be baptized with the Holy Spirit not many days from now" (Acts 1:4-5 NKJV).
>
> But you shall receive power when the Holy Spirit has come upon you; and you shall be witnesses to Me in Jerusalem, and in all Judea and Samaria, and to the end of the earth (Acts 1:8 NKJV).

I feel like I need to make it clear how important it is to understand the difference between the physical and spiritual transformation that takes place during salvation. If we understand this, it makes it so much easier to accept that Christians can be demonized. Your spirit man is untouched by demons, and after it is born again (born of the spirit), it can and should be filled with the Holy Spirit!

It is equally important to know that the only requirement for salvation is repentance, which we know is to believe in your heart and confess with your mouth that Jesus is Lord (Romans 10:9). This means that at any point of your Christian life, if you are pursuing the things of God and fearing Him, if you died you would go to heaven because your spirit man is born of God. The saved soul continues in its pursuit of holiness till Jesus comes again, so it's the soul of a man, not the spirit of a man, that is in constant battle with the powers of darkness.

The great news is that demons cannot stop you from receiving salvation, but they can hinder every step you take *as a Christian*. When something is dead there is no access to it—before salvation our spirit man is dead, so demons are unable to enter this part of a man. It therefore makes sense that the only part of a person demons have access to is the flesh, the soul man, because that is the part of man that remained alive even after the fall in the garden.

I believe when we begin to acknowledge that believers can have demons, freedom will mean freedom! When we read scriptures such as "*Therefore if the Son makes you free, you shall be free indeed*" in John 8:36 (NKJV), while we may believe it's the truth, so many of us do not experience the "free indeed" part. Yes, we have freedom from the sentence of a lost eternity, but even after we accept Jesus as our Lord and Savior, many of us still feel bound and not completely free. We could argue that it's a case of renewing the mind, and I agree that this is a most important part of experiencing true freedom. I also want to say here that working out our salvation means crucifying the flesh. Many times, people will ask for deliverance, thinking that their ungodly behavior is a demon, when it's just their flesh man unwilling to submit to the word of God. Almost the whole chapter in Galatians 5 refers to walking in freedom by dying to the flesh:

And those who are Christ's have crucified the flesh with its passions and desires (Galatians 5:24 NKJV).

But to my point here, I am referring to those who get born again who have brought those demons with them from their past lives unknowingly attached to their flesh. They didn't leave at the point of salvation because the saved person didn't even know that they were there! There is only *one* way to get rid of those demons and that is to cast them out. This is exactly what Jesus did when He was on earth. It's the instruction He gave to His disciples during the great commission in Mark 16:17, and it's the same instruction we are given today, which we must do in His Name!

We can read numerous stories in the New Testament of demons that were cast out of people. Most of the accounts use the word *possessed* with demons; however, the Greek word is *daimonion,* which means "demonized, oppressed, to occupy, to seize, to rob, to impoverish, to ruin." This makes so much more sense and gives us a greater understanding in knowing that this is what demons come to do. They rob us of our God-given personalities and character traits, they occupy our bodies and minds, they seize what rightfully belongs to us, and they cause poverty and lack to manifest in our lives.

We should be confident that possession doesn't take place in the spirit of a person before salvation because we now understand that the spirit of a person is dead, and demons cannot possess something that is dead! This is the whole reason we are separated from God in the first place—Satan destroyed this supernatural relationship in the garden. Man's spirit, which was made perfect, was the part of Adam and Eve that communicated with God in the garden, and when God said to Adam and Eve that they would die if they ate from the tree of knowledge, He was referring to their spiritual death, not their physical death. Separation from their relationship with God meant death, something they would only experience if they sinned. We know it was a spiritual death because after they sinned, the word tells us in Genesis 5:5 that Adam went on to live until he was 930 years old! Sin didn't immediately kill the body; it immediately killed the spirit. The only reason man's days were cut short was because of the wickedness of his heart; God could not allow man to live so long in this state. He put a stop to the long life man once had and brought it right down to 120 years!

> *And the Lord said, "My Spirit shall not strive with man forever, for he is indeed flesh; yet his days shall be one hundred and twenty years"* (Genesis 6:3 NKJV).

I want to make it clear that to be truly free we need three things: salvation, deliverance, and the word of God. The word *deliverance* means "salvation, liberation, acquittal, extrication, redemption, release, rescue, saving." It's interesting that the word for "save" in the scripture in James 1:21 (referring to the implanted word saving your soul) is the word *sozo* in Greek,

which means "saved, made whole, restored, healed, preserved, and delivered"!

We can easily say that the implanted word is able to save, make whole, restore, heal, preserve, and deliver our souls! *This* is the importance of the word of God and how it transforms our soul man. We can actually be delivered and set free many times by reading the word of God because it has transforming power for the believer. The word is God's voice, it's the acts of the Holy Spirit, and it's the demonstration of God's power. In Hebrews 4:12 (NKJV) we are told:

> *For the word of God is living and powerful, and sharper than any two-edged sword, piercing even to the division of soul and spirit, and of joints and marrow, and is a discerner of the thoughts and intents of the heart.*

When we are born again, the word feeds both our spirit and soul man, it transforms our soul man through revelation, and it's able to shift and remove demonic influences out of our lives.

Many believers struggle with the thought that Christians can have demons because they believe you are delivered the moment the prayer of salvation is prayed. I agree that some are delivered in this way, and I have heard many testimonies of people who have experienced this. The addictions they had to certain things stopped the moment they accepted Jesus Christ as their Lord and Savior. Addictions to nicotine, alcohol, drugs, swearing, and cussing were miraculously taken away. If this has happened to you or you know someone who experienced this, praise God, this is truly awesome and a testimony of God's

goodness! I really wish this could happen for everyone, but most times the things people need to be delivered from are more than outward addictions that can be seen, and I believe this is a key to understanding why deliverance of demonic spirits is necessary for many believers after they get born again.

The word says in James 5:16 (NASB):

> *Confess your sins to one another, and pray for one another so that you may be healed.*

The confession of sin sets people free. It brings both emotional and physical healing, and when we pray the prayer of salvation it includes repenting of our sin, which is why for some people when they get saved, they get delivered and set free all in one go! They can acknowledge not only their sin of unbelief but also the sin they know they have been committing, and instantly there is healing and deliverance because confession of sin sets us free.

The reason many who get born again still struggle with the same issues they had when they were in the world is that it's not so much the sin they personally committed, but sin that was committed *against* them. Let me explain it by giving you an illustration about car insurance, which may seem a little strange, but it really speaks to how unfair the whole thing is.

In the UK, when you get your car insured you must answer a long series of questions. Most of the questions are related to your driving history, but then they will also ask you questions that seem more related to the environment around you. They will ask what type of area you live in, where will you park your car when you are not using it, will it be parked somewhere

different at night from the daytime, will you take it to work, what will you be using it for, will anyone else be driving it? Many questions seem irrelevant, but then they will take all the information you have provided and work out how much it will cost you to insure your car. Seems straightforward, right?

When the price comes back it sometimes doesn't make any sense, especially if you know you have been a careful driver and have not had any accidents or speeding tickets. They calculate the cost not by how you have driven that year but by your driving history. If you have had an accident in the past, whether it was your fault or not, if someone has bumped into you, you will incur the cost for their mistake. They will use any misdemeanors you may have had as far back as five years. They will then check to see if there have been any recent vehicles stolen or car accidents in your area where you live and work and use that information also to determine the cost you should pay. Many times, you will end up paying a higher premium because of circumstances outside of your control rather than what you have personally been responsible for! The cost of car insurance in the UK, therefore, is calculated by the driving standards and habits of motorists around you, and based on what others have done, you end up paying the price!

This is the same scenario when it comes to deliverance. It's not so much that we have sinned, but it is sin people have committed against us. It's sin that has taken place in the home we grew up in. Its sinful behavior from our ancestors and relatives that are in our family bloodline. It is also words, declarations, agreements, covenants spoken over us—so many things that are completely out of our personal control! This is where demons get in. These are the open doors to our lives where they enter and these are the reasons they stay because we only know to repent for sin we have committed, not sin that's been committed against us, around us, or before we were ever born.

In Chapter 3, I wrote about the doors that demons enter through, and even how they enter from as early as in our mother's womb. When we've experienced trauma, fear, physical, emotional, or sexual abuse, none of these experiences are things we can repent of because we didn't do it to ourselves. Repentance brings deliverance, so how can we be delivered if we have experiences in our lives that have opened the door to demons through no fault of our own?

Understanding this makes it so much easier to recognize how demons can "possess" people. They occupy what doesn't belong to them. They steal what rightfully belongs to us, and they destroy the good things in our lives that we should be experiencing as believers.

The scripture I love to quote is John 10:10 (NKJV): "*The thief does not come except to steal, and to kill, and to destroy. I have come that they may have life, and that they may have it more abundantly.*" *Abundant* means "ample, bountiful, copious, generous, rich, sufficient, overflowing, plenteous, cup runs over"! Do you know being born again means that we should be living this abundant life? It is ours; Christ paid the price so that we could live this type of life right now here on earth.

I want to draw your attention to the first part of the scripture: "the thief comes *only*." Who is the thief? Satan! The scripture says he *only* comes to steal, kill, and destroy, which means his intention is solely to kill you, steal from you, and destroy you! If he can't kill you, even though you may get born again, he will try to steal all that rightfully belongs to you. If that doesn't stop you, he will then try to destroy you, your family, your possessions. *This is why he is on earth!* To take what he wishes was his. He doesn't want you to live the life God has promised you, and he tries with all his might to convince you that God doesn't want you to live that life either. He thinks, *If I can oppress them long enough and they don't know it's me, then they will lose their faith in God, they will stay the same, and I will stop them being effective as a Christian.* He loves to make God look bad, and to be honest, when I see Christians who are walking in defeat, have low self-esteem, have no money, don't know what to do with their life, it does make God look bad.

For some Christians, it's obvious that they have demons. Everyone can see it in their behavior, in their speech, and through their lifestyle, but many people don't realize this attack is in their life because they love the Lord, they are filled with the Holy Spirit, they know who they are in Christ, and they are even in a good church that operates in the power of the Holy Spirit. I know what you are thinking right now—*is there hope for any of us? How do I know if I have this in my life?* Well, I always explain it this way—it's like having a weighted blanket on you. If you have ever owned one, you will know what I'm talking about. They are designed to make you feel secure when you sleep or when you are resting because they are extremely heavy and prevent you from fidgeting or moving around. They are not designed to just throw around your shoulders to take off the chill if you fancy an evening stroll. Yes, you can get up and walk with them if you have a lot of strength, but they are purposely designed to weigh you down. If you were to try any kind of vigorous exercise with the weighted blanket over your shoulders, you would become exhausted very quickly.

When demons are present in your life, it's like walking around with a weighted blanket over you. You can still walk, but it's at a slow pace. You can still get to where you are going, but everything just seems such hard work. Nothing happens quickly, and you are exhausted at the end of it. Many people live this kind of Christian walk believing that this is just the way it is. Why? Because in general, everything seems to be fine; however, I always ask the question, "But are you living the abundant life promised in John 10:10?" It's crazy how we just put up with stuff that we know is not God's plan or best for our lives. It's like we are aware Satan is stealing from us, but we don't know how he's getting in. Let me reiterate—*abundance* means ample, bountiful, copious, generous, rich, sufficient, overflowing, plenteous, the cup runs over!

Christians need to be delivered more than ever! We must recognize that if we have demons, we need to be delivered (salvation, liberation, acquittal, extrication, redemption, release, rescue) from them and refuse to allow Satan to steal, kill, or destroy what rightfully belongs to us. Jesus said He came to give us life and life in abundance. *This* is how God purposed for us to live. When a Christian is delivered from demonic spirits, revival takes place on the inside of them because they start to see and hear clearly. The fog is lifted, the doubt is gone, they feel as light as a feather, and they are aware of the presence of the Holy Spirit in their life more than ever. The hunger for the word and the desire to be in God's presence increases a hundredfold!

Can you imagine if every Christian that needed deliverance was delivered? We would be in revival in every church, every house group, and every family!

CHAPTER 6

IT'S NOT POSSIBLE WITHOUT THE ANOINTING
IT CANNOT BE FAKED!

I OFTEN SAY THERE ARE MORE DEMONS ATTENDING CHURCH than actual people because where there are people, there are demons, and very rarely will there be just one demon per person! If a demon has found an open door in someone's life, he will jar that door open for all his demon friends to enter. Demons have no issue with attending church if they can hide in "their person," and if the person doesn't realize they are hosting demons, then they will put up no defense.

I remember a visiting minister commenting that he liked that our church wasn't too dark, but he just wasn't keen on the heavy black curtains that we were hanging on the white walls! He said, "You know demons like the dark, don't you?" His comment stopped me in my tracks. It was the first time I truly realized that the physical atmosphere we create in our sanctuaries makes a difference! I'm not specifically commenting on churches' décor or what color they choose to decorate their walls with, but it should make us think. Who do we have

in mind when we are putting up our fixtures and fittings and painting the walls? Who or what are we attracting into our gathering places?

Demons literally love the dark, and that's how they gain access to us in the first place—things that are done in the dark, behind closed doors, secrets that we don't let anyone know about, hidden things. Demons are at their most active in dark atmospheres, because here they are left unchallenged, ruling what they believe is their territory, the darkness, whether it be people or places. That's why nightclubs and music concerts are a favorite place for them. They go into overdrive in these atmospheres, especially when there is alcohol and drugs on the menu. If you've ever been to a venue like this, you will know what I'm talking about. We all know that nightclubs are a breeding ground for sexual promiscuity, aggression, violence, drunkenness. This is why I can't get my head around why many of our churches seem to model their sanctuaries on this style of building. They have black walls floor to ceiling and the only way to bring light into the atmosphere is from the lighting rig fixed with hundreds of artificial lights. I get that it looks better on livestream when you can control the lighting of a room, but I also know for a fact that the presence, anointing, and move of the Holy Spirit can permeate a camera lens regardless of how cool the building looks. It's His presence we need and it's His atmosphere we want people to experience, not our man-made atmospheric "vibey" concert-style church meeting.

Maybe I *am* saying that how we decorate our churches should be more to welcome the presence of God instead of the presence of people! Yes, we want to make our churches

welcoming, we want them to look good, but we don't want the décor to be so dark that demons feel it's like home away from home for them. The most important atmosphere to create, of course, is the spiritual one. We all know that you can have the most holy-looking church building with stained glass windows, with a whole heap of religious demons in the corner and void of the anointing and the presence of the Holy Spirit.

Please hear me—I'm truly not having a dig at churches that like their sanctuaries to look good. Our own sanctuary looks good, and we have purposely made it that way to welcome people. We love excellence, but our priority, above everything else, should be to make it welcoming to the Holy Spirit. The anointing can be anywhere because we carry the anointing; however, a space that makes the Holy Spirit feel comfortable and welcome is one where His manifestation will always be present.

What is the anointing? Well, it's the visible sign or atmospheric presence of the Holy Spirit on a person or in a place. It's His manifest presence that is felt, experienced, or even seen. It permeates the atmosphere and changes people instantly! There have been hundreds of testimonies in which people have experienced the anointing in the form of the glory cloud descending. It appears like a mist, and everyone touched by that mist, His glory, is saved, healed, or delivered. When the anointing is this strong in a place, people have reported seeing gold dust and rain falling. It's like God standing right next to you and bringing heaven's atmosphere into the room! I will explain it further as we move on.

It's the anointing that causes demons to manifest, which is why sadly they can attend many churches unnoticed. They are

present during the worship, they are present during the word, they listen to the announcements, they enjoy a tea or coffee afterward, and then they leave the same way they came in—unnoticed, hidden, and very comfortable inhabiting "their person." Remember in the word of God how Jesus would be walking along and there would be a demon-possessed person and they would just start to cry out when they saw Him? It wasn't because they heard about Him or His physical stature made them afraid—it was because He continually walked in the anointing, and that anointing literally exposed the demons on the inside of the people. It wasn't the people themselves crying out; it was the demons. They couldn't hide because the Holy Spirit's presence on Jesus exposed them and forced them out into the open.

The atmosphere we create in our churches is so important, and I must admit that many churches do look more like nightclubs than sanctuaries. A sanctuary by definition is a holy place, a harbor, a haven, an oasis, a refuge and shelter. It provides protection, a shield, a safe house. When people come into our sanctuaries, they should be able to get free from everything that has hindered them. When those demons enter with people, they should start getting really uncomfortable, so much so that they begin to cry out and expose themselves. Even when people are around you, if you are walking in the anointing of God, demons should be uncomfortable being around you. Perhaps some of you have experienced this before and have never realized that it's the anointing on you that is causing a person to act weird or uncomfortable in your presence.

When those demons manifested on seeing Jesus, He dealt with them straightaway with no fuss. They obeyed Him instantly. I detest giving Satan any glory or giving his demons any room to show off or express themselves during church services, but quite often this cannot be avoided because of the anointing that is present. Every week we invite people to come to the altar; sometimes it's during the service, but it will always be at the end of the service. We keep an open altar, so people are free to come forward for whatever they may need prayer for. I can always guarantee there will be someone who will need deliverance ministry, whether they know it or not. I am very grateful that we have deliverance ministers within our ministry team who know how to pray for people.

We are also very careful to protect people when they come to the altar, so our prayer team will often form a wall around those being delivered to protect both them and the congregation. It can be quite a shock to see the manifestation that often comes when someone is being delivered—shouting, shrieking, coughing, swearing, or physical manifestations of kicking, rolling about on the floor, or being sick. We've seen most things, but I am wise enough to know by now that I probably haven't seen everything, and when I think I've seen it all, a new manifestation will rear its ugly head to surprise me! You can imagine among lots of people being prayed for, it's not always easy to pay full attention in the way that is needed to cast out every demon present in a person. Demons love the limelight; they love to disrupt church services, so quite consciously we will close some manifestations down as quickly as possible, or we will take them to a side room to continue. We do this as discreetly as we can, and many times we will invite the person to come to a private deliverance session as soon as they are able.

This is my preferred way of delivering people. It's private, it's a safe environment, it's not limited to time, and it's purpose-driven to seeing the person completely set free.

It's interesting—as Christians there are many things you can do without the anointing. I'm not suggesting it's a good thing, but you know what I mean. People preach, lead worship, pray, and they can get away with it because maybe what they are saying or singing or praying is the word and it sounds good plus they have natural giftings given to them by God. Our churches can get away with having good services because we are saying and doing all the right things expected in a meeting. One thing you *cannot* do, however, is cast out or expose a demon without the anointing of God! Demons can smell you a mile off. They know if you are the real deal, and they know if your church is the real deal or if it's a place they can attend unhindered! Remember the incident that happened with the disciples in the book of Matthew:

> *"Lord, have mercy on my son, for he is an epileptic and suffers severely; for he often falls into the fire and often into the water. So I brought him to your disciples, but they could not cure him."*
>
> *Then Jesus answered and said, "O faithless and perverse generation, how long shall I be with you? How long shall I bear with you? Bring him here to Me." And Jesus rebuked the demon, and it came out of him; and the child was cured from that very hour.*
>
> *Then the disciples came to Jesus privately and said, "Why could we not cast it out?" So Jesus said to*

them, "Because of your unbelief; for assuredly, I say to you, if you have faith as a mustard seed, you will say to this mountain, 'Move from here to there,' and it will move; and nothing will be impossible for you. However, this kind does not go out except by prayer and fasting" (Matthew 17:15-21 NKJV).

The disciples lacked a few things—faith, authority, and the anointing of the Holy Spirit. When Jesus sent them out originally in Luke 9:1, it says He gave them power and authority to cast out demons and to cure diseases, but this time it was different. They were working on their own, and they lacked faith and the anointing even in all that they had learned from Jesus. You can tell this was the case because the scripture says that they came to Him privately. They were probably embarrassed; they were supposed to be these great disciples of Jesus who had been present for all the miracles. Prior to this incident they had been sent out themselves and had been able to cast out demons and heal the sick, but this time, when faced with this demon, they became powerless.

Jesus was not impressed, but His response was interesting. First of all, He called them a faithless and perverse generation! Gosh, what a statement! That must have been difficult for them to hear. I don't believe Jesus was being mean to the disciples; He was just frustrated that they had taken their eyes off the One who did the miracles, the One who was the source of the power that they had! Their faith may have been in themselves to cast the demon out; after all, they were Jesus' disciples and everyone knew that there was an expectation that they were the boys to get the job done, but they forgot that the only reason they had

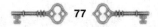

power was because Jesus gave it to them, and it was His Name that the demons were subject to!

What did He mean when He said, "*This kind does not go out except by prayer and fasting*"? I believe He was referring to spending time in the presence of the Lord. Maybe this is why He was frustrated with them as well. They had spent so much time with Him, they should have known whatever they did was for the glory of God, not themselves. We all know that when we have spent time praying and fasting, we become closer to the Lord, we love Him more, we feel stronger, more focused, full of faith, and we become more sensitive to the voice of the Holy Spirit. This is why in Acts 1:4 and 8 He told the disciples that they must wait for the promise of the Father and the power of the Holy Spirit to come. He knew what they needed so they would never doubt whose authority they were walking in or lack faith or go out without the anointing again.

It's the same with us—without the Holy Spirit we cannot cast out demons. It's not our power or our name that demons respond to. Without intimacy with the Lord, it can also become us using His Name to make ourselves look good. The glory belongs to God, not us. Jesus only ever did what He was told to do by the Father, and it was *all* to bring glory to His Father! If our church meetings are not centered on the presence of God, the love of God, and His anointing then people will remain bound with demons, still attending church, still loving the Lord, but living a fraction of the abundant life that has been promised to them.

News flash! Satan is not afraid of churches, whether they be large or small. He's not afraid of megachurch ministries, he's not afraid of new cutting-edge churches, he's not even afraid

of famous apostles, prophets, evangelists, pastors, or teachers. He doesn't like them; in fact, he hates all of them and works tirelessly to destroy them all, *but* there's one thing that causes him to fear and tremble and quake in his boots, and that's all the above people and/or places filled with and operating in the anointing of the Holy Spirit, motivated by the love of God!

Why does the anointing make the difference? Because the anointing is God's presence. It's as if He is standing there Himself. The anointing is God's agreement. It's His anointing and His anointing only that sets the captive free and undoes every ounce of work Satan has inflicted in a person's life.

> *The Spirit of the Lord God is upon me, because the Lord has anointed me to bring good news to the afflicted; He has sent me to bind up the broken-hearted, to proclaim liberty to captives and freedom to prisoners* (Isaiah 61:1 NASB).

Again, in Luke 4:18-19 (NKJV) this is Jesus declaring those powerful words from Isaiah and telling the Jews that this scripture was being fulfilled in their presence.

> *The Spirit of the Lord is upon Me, because He has anointed Me to preach the gospel to the poor; He has sent Me to heal the brokenhearted, to proclaim liberty to the captives and recovery of sight to the blind, to set at liberty those who are oppressed; to proclaim the acceptable year of the Lord.*

The anointing breaks chains, it brings freedom, it releases people from the grasp of Satan, it destroys his bonds that bind people, it brings healing, and it removes his demons from people's lives.

> *It was for freedom that Christ set us free; therefore keep standing firm and do not be subject again to a yoke of slavery* (Galatians 5:1 NASB).
>
> *How God anointed Jesus of Nazareth with the Holy Spirit and with power, who went about doing good and healing all who were oppressed by the devil, for God was with Him* (Acts 10:38 NKJV.)

In the Old Testament in the book of Leviticus 10 and 21, the anointing was a public sign that you were separated and consecrated for God's purpose, that you carried out His instructions on His behalf and you were trusted to steward His will. It was a sign that His presence was with you. It was only appointed people such as the prophets, priests, and kings God Himself chose who could receive His anointing to carry out His work. The oil they used was specifically made for this purpose. Instructions were given on what ingredients to use to make this holy anointing oil, how they should make it, and what utensils they should use. This was no ordinary oil they would use for cooking; this was God's oil, His holy and sanctified oil that they would rub and daub over a person, object, or building specified by God. It was a serious offense to use this special anointing oil for anything other than holy consecration, and if they did use it for something else, it would result in the offender being cut off from his people. It was not taken lightly; the fear and awe of

God was meant to be on anyone carrying out His instructions regarding the anointing oil.

In the New Testament, if we are born again and filled with the Holy Spirit, we all carry the anointing to do His will. It's no longer an outward consecration but an inward consecration and separation of the heart. We all receive the commission from Jesus in Mark 16:15,17-18 (NKJV):

> *Go into all the world and preach the gospel to every creature…and these signs will follow those who believe: In My name they will cast out demons; they will speak with new tongues; they will take up serpents; and if they drink anything deadly, it will by no means hurt them; they will lay hands on the sick, and they will recover.*

When a believer knows who they are in Christ and is anointed to operate in the power and authority that they have been given, Satan is frightened. When believers and churches prioritize spending time praying and fasting, living in the presence of the Lord, and loving Him and seeking His face and His purpose, they will see true freedom, liberty, abundance, and revival. I previously touched on the love of God because it is so connected with operating in the anointing and the casting out of demons. The whole reason God wants His people free is because He loves each one of us. His love is His driving force to rescue, save, and set us free. If all our churches operated like this, then demons would not be able to survive in this kind of atmosphere!

Let's get personal. Be honest with yourself—do you recognize that you have missed it in a few areas? Do you identify with the disciples and the mistake they made with trying to cast out a demon because of reputation or because they had been used in this area before and they were positive it should work again? Let me encourage you—our relationship with the Lord is key to seeing miracles take place through our hands. Even though we are all filled with His Spirit, the anointing of the Holy Spirit operates quite differently. Yes, we are anointed and set apart to do His will. We have dynamic power on the inside of us, but what separated Jesus was the anointing that was seen *on* Him. It was visible, but this type of anointing only comes with spending time *with* the Father.

My intimacy a month ago with the Lord will not carry me through the next six months. It is a daily consecration before Him, it is daily seeking His face, it is daily receiving instruction from the Holy Spirit. Why do you think Jesus hit the mark every time? He was constantly fellowshipping with His heavenly Father; you only have to read John 14–17 to know how much He loved His heavenly Father and did everything to please Him. It is such a beautiful couple of chapters in which He comforts His disciples but also reveals the relationship He has with the Father and Holy Spirit. This is what we must have to operate like He did! Everything we do must be motivated by the love of the Father to bring glory to His Name and to only do what the Holy Spirit instructs us to do. If this is our focus, the anointing will be present wherever we go!

Are you in a church that allows the Holy Spirit to guide the service? Do you sense the presence of God in the meetings, and is the worship and the preaching of the word anointed? In the last days, God specifically says that He is going to pour out His

Spirit on all flesh. I know the "last days" have technically been since the Day of Pentecost, but unless you have been on some desert island somewhere and have not been about for the last several years, you will know that we are in the last of the last days. It's not a probably or maybe; it's a definitely! If as a Christian you are trying to conduct your life without the anointing of the Holy Spirit and the presence of God, then you only have yourself to blame. God has not withheld anything from you, and in fact, the scriptures say in both Joel 2 and Luke 4 that His Spirit will be poured out on *all* flesh. He lists everyone— old men, young men, women, servants. Bear in mind in the Old Testament the anointing was so holy and sacred it was only reserved for the appointed few! In the last days, God states that this will not be the case; His anointing, which means His holy presence, His agreement, will be available to everyone!

It's time to get serious, and it may be time to reposition yourself. Jesus is coming back very soon, and in these last days it is only the anointing and the power of the Holy Spirit working through us that will set the captives free. This is our responsibility—to keep our eyes focused on Jesus and more importantly to be free ourselves! Yes, you can still be used if you are carrying demons around with you, but as we have already read in Chapter 4, we want to live our lives with no heavy weights holding us back, dragging us down, or making it difficult for us to run our race! Being free to do all that God has called us to do, as I have just stated, is our responsibility, and now that we know this truth, the truth known is able to set us free!

CHAPTER 7

COUNSELING
AND DELIVERANCE
KNOWING THE
DIFFERENCE

*For God has not given us a spirit of fear, but of power
and of love and of a sound mind.*

—2 TIMOTHY 1:7 NKJV

CHRISTIANS SOMETIMES TURN TO WORLDLY COUNSELING
to deal unknowingly with spiritual issues because they
struggle to believe that they can be demonized or that the
church has the power to help them. This is especially true when
it comes to mental health. Many believe healing in this area
can only come from the world. They feel that the church just
doesn't understand. There are many good counseling methods
that work for people; I would never want to discount them or
the great therapists that are out there, but sadly this is a miscon-
ception. Counseling that the believer receives from the world
can only ever address the emotional issues of the trauma they
have experienced.

Many Christians believe the only way through their mental health struggle or trauma is to seek professional counseling, therapy, or medication in the world. I want to make a couple of points in this next chapter to hopefully differentiate and show you the differences between counseling, medication, and deliverance and why I believe deliverance is necessary in these cases—not always opposed to, but sometimes alongside counseling. I will say, however, on most occasions deliverance is enough on its own, and when it's not we find it is more to do with a person preferring to rely on a "system" or "method" of healing to get free rather than relying fully on God and His power. This may sound judgmental against a person who has sought help from the world, but it is not meant to be. I can only speak from experience, and in truth, I totally understand and "get" why people put more faith in professional, worldly counseling and therapy than the church. However, for too long the church has not operated in the power we have been given, and as a result, has ended up hurting broken people even more because of our poor theology and ignorance when it comes to mental health and trauma (which is why Christians turn to the world for help!). When people have complex trauma, we believe and hope a simple prayer over them will make it all go away. When it doesn't, we put the ownership back on the person and blame them for not receiving our ill-given advice or our one-time prayer properly!

We must recognize that people, including Christians, who have gone through or are going through any type of trauma need to be listened too. Our flippant responses of "You just have to forgive the person who abused you," "It's under the blood,"

"You need to forget the past," "It's time to move on," makes a person even more traumatized! Just knowing how demons operate should give us a clear understanding that it's impossible to just "get over it," especially when we understand the connection between epigenetics and trauma, which I believe Satan has clearly used to distort the paths and purposes God has designed for our life.

Obviously, the above statements of forgiving our abusers are correct and biblical when used in the right context. The word of God works—it saves, heals, delivers, and restores—but I have witnessed many Christians hurt with the way the church has dealt with their pain. One lady who came for deliverance recounted that so many times she was not listened to and when she would say that she struggled to move on, she was quoted every scripture you could think of that was related to forgiveness. When I made a series of programs talking about sex and the church, one of the episodes dealt with the church's response to abuse. I had a couple of guests on who gave their personal experiences when it came to seeking help and healing from within the church. Both had terrible experiences that left them feeling even more guilt-ridden and shamed because they couldn't forgive those who hurt and violated them. Again, this led to both getting help from outside of the church. It was the familiar response of having to forgive their perpetrators and that they needed to just move on that drove them outside of the very place that has been equipped by God through the Holy Spirit to heal them! No one once ministered to them in deliverance or helped them move on outside of a simple prayer and some suspect counseling! Unless we understand and believe in the power of deliverance and the role it plays in dealing with past trauma, we will always be trying to fix people with a one-dimensional mindset, and this will never be able to help people heal body, soul, and spirit.

I also believe many times in the church when we pray or try to counsel people who have experienced abuse, we try to come up with the quickest solution. We want to fix the person without any investment into their life. We don't take the time to listen to them as we should. This is not what Jesus did, and He is our example to follow. When He encountered the woman at the well in John 4, He went out of His way to minister to her. He knew her background, He knew her sorrow, and He knew her sins, yet He took time to talk with her and not at her. The result was that she received freedom and a new life that transformed not only herself but her entire village. Her life changed dramatically forever from the counsel Jesus gave to her!

So again, I understand why Christians turn to other sources for answers. The saddest thing is that the church does have the power, it has the answers, and it has the means to turn lives around. Jesus is the answer, He led by example, and He gave us His Holy Spirit. He expects us to operate the way He did, with compassion, love, and power! Remember when He was speaking to His disciples and instructing them on what was to come, He made this statement:

> *Most assuredly, I say to you, he who believes in Me, the works that I do he will do also; and greater works than these he will do, because I go to My Father. And whatever you ask in My name, that I will do, that the Father may be glorified in the Son. If you ask*

anything in My name, I will do it (John 14:12-14 NKJV).

Heal the sick, cleanse the lepers, raise the dead, cast out demons. Freely you have received, freely give (Matthew 10:8 NKJV).

Jesus didn't just counsel or speak to people, He spent most of His time healing them by casting out demons! He said we too would do this kind of work and even greater!

People should be coming to the church for every type of healing and not going to the world. We have Jesus' authority to use to deliver people, and then we have the Holy Spirit who not only anoints us to do the work, but He is our counselor. He has given us His gifts of healing, miracles, faith, words of wisdom, words of knowledge, discernment of spirits, the gift of prophecy, gift of tongues, and the interpretation of tongues. Surely these gifts are enough to deliver someone from their past, bringing them safely through to the other side healed and whole and thriving in their soul.

My aim in this chapter is to hopefully bring clarity and comfort to those of you who have had a bad experience in church, to restore your faith that God has provided everything needed in His house to heal all your wounds, both inside and out, mental and emotional! I also hope all of us will gain understanding in the words that I have written when it comes to the differences between counseling and deliverance and why both may be necessary for true freedom. I'm praying for everyone reading this that you will find the answers that you didn't even know you needed!

First, I want to say regarding my own church, we have a wonderful counseling team. Some are counselors by profession, others are part of the pastoral care team. They have all been through training and they will spend as long as it takes to bring someone through to victory. I believe wholeheartedly in counseling, and it's something I spend a lot of time doing especially as part of the deliverance ministry. The Holy Spirit showed me quite clearly, however, through illustrations, the role that counseling plays when someone has gone through trauma of any kind. Counseling is physical therapy for the heart—it helps it to recover, it helps it to work again, it helps it to recognize what is good for it and what is bad. Deliverance is the operation—it physically removes all foreign objects, it cleans up the area that was damaged, it puts it back to its original state. You cannot have physical therapy before the operation because what was broken needs to be fixed and cleaned first.

Can you imagine, for instance, if you had a broken leg and a physical therapist tried to have you walk on it before you had surgery to realign the bones that had been broken? It would cause more damage and take longer to see any possible results because the bones would be out of their original position. Without the surgery, maybe over time the leg would heal naturally, but it wouldn't heal the way it was originally designed, and you could never use it the same way again, which would affect every part of your daily life. It just doesn't make any sense in the natural to have it that way around, and it's the same in the spirit with deliverance and counseling. Deliverance *must* come first to get rid of all those demons oppressing, binding, and preventing you from moving on. The soul must be cleaned up first.

As three-part beings—body, soul, and spirit—every part of us is affected when we endure trauma, so it stands to reason that counseling alone will not completely heal a person. It cannot be our only answer because it just speaks to the problem from a natural standpoint with very little to no reference to the spiritual, and this is the problem when Christians seek professional help solely from the world. The world's insights and the world's wisdom cannot completely heal them. This is what God's word says about the knowledge we find in the world:

> *Don't let anyone capture you with empty philosophies and high-sounding nonsense that come from human thinking and from the spiritual powers of this world, rather than from Christ* (Colossians 2:8 NLT).

> *The message of the cross is foolish to those who are headed for destruction! But we who are being saved know it is the very power of God. As the Scriptures say, "I will destroy the wisdom of the wise and discard the intelligence of the intelligent." So where does this leave the philosophers, the scholars, and the world's brilliant debaters? God has made the wisdom of this world look foolish* (1 Corinthians 1:18-20 NLT).

I think I have already said enough so that you know I am not discounting counseling, therapy, or any other form of help for mental wellbeing that the world or even the church offers. What I am saying is that when you only try to deal with the natural part of a man, those demons that are the real cause of the

problem in the first place may lay low for a little while; but they will rear their heads up again at some point, and the person will still have to deal with those negative emotions even after they have gone through numerous amounts of counseling or therapy. Most people who go through counseling are aware of "triggers" that take them right back to square one, and they are encouraged to recognize the triggers before their emotions take over.

Counseling does have a significant part to play in the deliverance ministry. It's how you get to the root of the problem, but once the root is found the only way to deal with it is to dig it up and cast out what has been planted, because what has been planted is demonic. The power in deliverance will eradicate those emotions at the root because they are demons, so the person never has to worry about triggers or if they are going to break down and go back to their old self because that old self has been set free! The demons who were the root cause have been cast out. This is the biggest difference, and we must acknowledge it in the church. We must stop trying to put band-aids on open wounds when we have been given the correct instructions and procedures to clean up the deepest of wounds and bring healing and freedom to the sufferer, body, soul, and spirit.

> *How God anointed Jesus of Nazareth with the Holy Spirit and with power, who went about doing good and healing all who were oppressed by the devil, for God was with Him* (Acts 10:38 NKJV).

The church must wake up. There is healing in deliverance!

The second point I want to make is regarding medication for mental health issues. I am not against it and would never

encourage anyone to stop taking prescribed medication unless they are fully healed or delivered. However, there is a problem with medication when it's to do with mental health issues and depression. The medication suppresses *your* emotions and feelings, *not* the demon's! Have you ever wondered why the moment you stop taking the medication, you slip back into depression again? If you believe the medication is the answer, you can become addicted to it without ever realizing the real answer and solution to the problem is deliverance! Every mental health issue of the mind has its roots in the demonic. God promises to give us a sound mind, but Satan's quest is always to attack our mind, because our mind is the filtration system to our heart. So again, I am just reiterating that the world cannot help you heal from something that is a spiritual problem!

Medication dulls the senses; it can even put you in a trance-like state. You may be physically present in a room, but it can be difficult to be emotionally in the room! Medication becomes addictive when you rely on it. Again, you cannot fix a spiritual problem with natural methods, and medication is a worldly method. I'm not saying it's wrong in all circumstances, but when using it to treat trauma, God has already provided the best way. The medications that doctors prescribe for stress, anxiety, depression, and suicidal thoughts are synthetic chemicals that imitate our brain's natural stimulants for wellbeing, good moods, and emotions. God imparted His knowledge to us when He created Adam and Eve in His image in the beginning, and even though man fell, God allowed us to retain all that knowledge and wisdom, which includes the ability to create. Scientists are very clever at copying how God physically made us. They have learned how our bodies and brains function and respond to difficult and traumatic events in our lives. If we didn't have an alternative then we would have to rely on scientists and doctors, but as born-again believers we know the provision God has made to heal us in our minds and our bodies is perfect, and it is so much better than any medication or remedy that the world can offer us.

I have ministered to so many Christians who rely on prescribed medication to prevent them falling into depression. Many have had a lifetime of struggle from trauma or a series of difficult events that have taken place in their lives. They become very nervous about trusting God completely to heal them. They will receive prayer but will continue to trust more in the medication that the doctor has prescribed. If Satan or his demons can convince us that we need the medication to be normal, then to an extent he has control over us, even as Christians. The word of God clearly states:

> For God has not given us a spirit of fear, but of power and of love and of a sound mind (2 Timothy 1:7 NKJV).

> For "who has known the mind of the Lord that he may instruct Him?" But we have the mind of Christ (1 Corinthians 2:16 NKJV).

When depression hits, it starts with the thoughts in the mind, and we know this is Satan's favorite battleground against humans. This is where he attacks us every single time. He uses suggestive thoughts, negative thoughts, suicidal thoughts, wicked thoughts, angry thoughts—all are inserted into our minds, which is why those scriptures give us hope!

We are specifically taught by the apostle Paul in 2 Corinthians 10:3-6 (NKJV):

> *For though we walk in the flesh, we do not war according to the flesh. For the weapons of our warfare are not carnal but mighty in God for pulling down strongholds, casting down arguments and every high thing that exalts itself against the knowledge of God, bringing every thought into captivity to the obedience of Christ, and being ready to punish all disobedience when your obedience is fulfilled.*

The instruction is perfectly clear—we are to cast down *every* negative thought that comes into our mind or that contradicts the word of God.

I believe that God has given us a way and keys in dealing with the onslaught of the enemy. God didn't leave us to get on with things after the fall. He already had a plan in place by sending Jesus and then sending the Holy Spirit. We were not supposed to experience death or destruction; nor were we created to have to deal with fear, failure, guilt, or shame. God made a way and gave us supernatural strategies as well as His word to overcome all the works of the enemy in our lives. When problems come, we should first and foremost turn to God and His word, because He has already made provision for these kinds of attacks, and we are to lean and rely on the Holy Spirit to lead us into freedom.

This is the pattern concerning the battle in the mind. Thoughts meditated on in the mind go down into the heart; the heart is our belief system, and so we will speak what's in the heart, which is whatever we believe. I've already said it in previous chapters, and again I quote the word of God in Proverbs 4:23 (NKJV): "*Keep your heart with all diligence, for out of it spring the issues of life.*" When what you believe in your heart seems true, real, or right, it will be the platform or foundation on how you live your life. Satan knows this. He loves to reprogram us through our mind so that we function and rely on his "answers" to our problems. It's like we unknowingly reach out to him via the world's system. This is why from the youngest age, he sends his demons to enter our lives at the points of tragedy, trauma, or abuse. If he can cause our foundation to be wrong and built on his lies and deception, then it will change the whole trajectory of the life God purposed for us. Jesus *is* our foundation:

> *For no other foundation can anyone lay than that which is laid, which is Jesus Christ* (1 Corinthians 3:11 NKJV).

I love the way the New Living Translation says it:

> *For no one can lay any foundation other than the one we already have—Jesus Christ.*

This is how Satan tries to rewrite history. He tried to alter the foundation from the beginning, and it's the same way when it comes to our individual lives. He has used this strategy for centuries!

A foundation is something that holds everything else up. It must be solid, concrete. It must be able to weather every storm! The dictionary describes it this way: "the basis or groundwork of anything: the moral foundation of both society and religion." Some of the synonyms used are *infrastructure, heart, bedrock, root, nuts and bolts, underpinning, reason.* Many of these words give us an understanding as to why non-believers are so blinded to the truth of the gospel. If their foundations are set up and orchestrated by Satan, then he can distort who they believe they are, their morals, the path their life takes. It also explains why many believers struggle even when they become born again! The wrong foundation (belief system) will always cause a problem, no matter how high you climb in your Christian faith. If the foundation is not built on Jesus, then your life will continually come crashing down. It may even be that your Christian walk will always remain mediocre. You love God and going to church but you never fully trust Him or His provision in your life.

> *Beloved, I pray that you may prosper in all things and be in health, just as your soul prospers* (3 John 1:2 NKJV).

God's desire is that we prosper in *all* things. We are to look to Him for our health, for our emotional wellbeing, for our physical and spiritual health. *Prosper* means "to blossom, to thrive, to increase, to bear fruit."

Whatever we may go through in life or the experiences we have already gone through, God has made provision both supernaturally and naturally for us to overcome it and live a life

of freedom that is promised in His word. It's not a quick fix, even with deliverance, and sometimes we must receive it more than once—His word in our life only takes effect if we put it into practice, if we believe in our hearts and speak it out with our mouths, if we capture thoughts that the enemy tries to plant in our minds and cast them down.

If we choose to take the world's route of counseling or medication, it works to a degree, but it doesn't remove the real problem, which can only be dug up and cast out through the ministry of deliverance at the root. Demons will not be counseled, and they will not be medicated; they thrive on our negative and confused emotions, which all along belong to them.

The world doesn't know any different. It has refused to acknowledge that we have a creator God. So, while they believe they have come up with all the scientific answers and think they are the clever ones, God just smiles. He doesn't take back the knowledge, which is His, because He loves His creation too much. He would ultimately rather us heal somehow than not at all.

CHAPTER 8

ORIGINS AND PURPOSE
HOW DEMONS ARRIVED ON EARTH

WE ALL KNOW SATAN IS EVIL AND THAT HE IS INTENT ON destroying mankind. But to understand his origins, we can read specifically in two scriptures in the Old Testament about the creation of Lucifer (his angelic name) and why he became an adversary of God and leader of a demonic army.

> *You were the seal of perfection, full of wisdom and perfect in beauty. You were in Eden, the garden of God; every precious stone was your covering: the sardius, topaz, and diamond, beryl, onyx, and jasper, sapphire, turquoise, and emerald with gold. The workmanship of your timbrels and pipes was prepared for you on the day you were created. You were the anointed cherub who covers; I established you; you were on the holy mountain of God; you walked back and forth in the midst of fiery stones. You were perfect in your ways from the day you were created, till iniquity was found in you* (Ezekiel 28:12-15 NKJV).

How you are fallen from heaven, O Lucifer, son of the morning! How you are cut down to the ground, you who weakened the nations! For you have said in your heart: "I will ascend into heaven, I will exalt my throne above the stars of God" (Isaiah 14:12-13 NKJV).

Lucifer really had everything. He was trusted and revered by the heavenly hosts. He was given one of the highest positions in the heavenly kingdom, anointed to worship, skilled in sound and music, and created beautifully in every way. Yet this wasn't enough for him.

He desired God's throne, believing that he was equal with God, and so the pride he had in his heart eventually became his downfall. Along with a third of the angels, which he led in rebellion toward God, He was thrown out of heaven. Satan has knowledge when it comes to God's kingdom; he spent eons in heaven with Him. He knows God, he understands the workings of the heavenly kingdom, and he is familiar with Michael and all the angelic warriors. He is intent on destroying everything God ever created, including us, and even though he is no match for God, he is relentless in his pursuit of victory. His influence in this world is reaching a tipping point; however, the battle has already been won through Jesus' victory on the cross. He will never win because that victory is ours, it belongs to us, but we must be present, active, and involved in these last days to enforce the victory that we have.

The scriptures are clear in several places in the New Testament when it refers to the unseen realm and how it operates in the heavenlies and on earth. We are also made aware of the

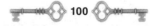

demonic forces that have resisted God's kingdom in the Old Testament, as shown clearly in the book of Daniel.

> *But the prince of the kingdom of Persia withstood me twenty-one days; and behold, Michael, one of the chief princes, came to help me, for I had been left alone there with the kings of Persia* (Daniel 10:13 NKJV).

Here we can read that there are both angelic and demonic princes operating in the heavenlies and that they war against one another when saints pray. The prince of Persia is referring to a principality or demonic "prince" that had control over the region. He was so powerful that Michael was sent for to help defeat him. Satan has discharged this army to take control over kingdoms, countries, and regions of the earth. His legal authority to do this came with the fall of man when he deceived Adam and Eve into sinning against God. Adam and Eve's one act of disobedience allowed Satan to take their authority away from them so that he could have dominion over the earth in their place.

There are ranks in Satan's army, it is vast, and it is ordered. He uses principalities and powers to influence and control nations and regions, he uses the rulers of darkness to infiltrate governments and organizations, and he uses the hosts of wickedness, or evil spirits, to harass and demonize individual people. From the scriptures in the New Testament, we understand the hierarchy of this dark kingdom.

> *For we do not wrestle against flesh and blood, but against principalities, against powers, against*

the rulers of the darkness of this age, against spiritual hosts of wickedness in the heavenly places (Ephesians 6:12 NKJV).

For by Him all things were created that are in heaven and that are on earth, visible and invisible, whether thrones or dominions or principalities or powers (Colossians 1:16 NKJV).

Having disarmed principalities and powers, He made a public spectacle of them, triumphing over them in it (Colossians 2:15 NKJV).

For I am persuaded that neither death nor life, nor angels nor principalities nor powers, nor things present nor things to come (Romans 8:38 NKJV).

The demonic realm has been active on earth for millennia, and there are a couple of interesting scriptures in the book of Colossians that I want to point out. First, in Colossians 1:16 it states that He, being God, created the visible and the invisible—meaning as well as us, He also created the principalities and powers, although we recognize that it wasn't in their evil form that He originally created them. These beings were not created by Satan, because Satan cannot create anything. All that God creates in its originality brings light and life, so we know these heavenly beings were once good until they chose to follow Satan who distorted, perverted, and destroyed the purpose God originally had for them. This is the same thing he does to us! This demonic spiritual army, led by Satan, tirelessly schemes and plots against God, His Kingdom, and His people.

Second, and this one makes me smile, it says in Colossians 2:15 that Satan, the principalities, and powers were completely

stripped of their legal authority in front of all the heavenly hosts. That means all of heaven was watching and witnessed their defeat! The destruction, chaos, and wickedness that they had brought on the earth without legal opposition had now ended abruptly because of Jesus' death, burial, and resurrection! Yes, they would continue in this destruction because they won't abide by God's laws, but now the tables had turned and God was and is raising up His own army that has the power and authority, by right of belief and acceptance of Jesus' sacrifice on the cross, to once again rebuke, cast down, cast out, dismantle, and destroy all the works of darkness! Jesus is our forerunner and greatest example!

> *For this purpose the Son of God was manifested, that He might destroy the works of the devil* (1 John 3:8 NKJV).
>
> *You have died with Christ, and he has set you free from the spiritual powers of this world* (Colossians 2:20 NLT).

So, from scripture we can understand where Satan, the principalities, and powers came from, but where exactly do the spirits that demonize people come from? Ephesians 6:12 mentions them in the list of heavenly beings, referring to them as spiritual hosts of wickedness. We sometimes refer to them as spirits because they are disembodied beings that roam the earth. We are all spirit beings, but as humans when our physical bodies die, our spirit man will vacate and leave the earth until the time, if we are believers, when we unite with Jesus and receive our glorified bodies. Demons do not want to leave the earth and so will search for bodies to inhabit so that they can stay!

We all know the story in Matthew 8:28-34 of the mad man of the Gadarenes. Remember how the demons begged Jesus to send them into the herd of swine instead of being sent to the abyss! They would go anywhere rather than leaving the earth. When I first started casting demons out of people, I thought I was dealing with some superior being in Satan's kingdom, but demons are the lowest rank in Satan's evil army and are subject not only to Satan, but to his principalities, his powers, and rulers of darkness. They literally are the lowest of the low in ranking. Many Christians are intimidated by even the mention of a demon, let alone a demon itself, but I want to encourage you that you are ranked way above the most evil and ugliest of demons! Just like the seventy who were sent out in Luke 10:17 (NKJV):

> *Then the seventy returned with joy, saying, "Lord, even the demons are subject to us in Your name."*

When they came back, they were rejoicing and marveling because the demons were subject to them when they used the name of Jesus! This is the same authority you carry as a child of God, and it outranks any jurisdiction or stronghold that any demon has.

There is no clear or absolute understanding of the origins of demons. There are several different viewpoints, but I want to give just two that are held by Christians. One view believed by many Jewish and Christian scholars is that demons are the spirits of the Nephilim, the race of giants found in Genesis 6. They were the offspring of the sons of God and the daughters

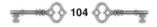

of men. The sons of God were some kind of heavenly beings with an evil agenda that took the daughters of men and had sexual intercourse with them, producing giants. This perverted and distorted God's human creation because the sons of God stepped outside of their natural domain.

> *And the angels who did not keep their proper domain, but left their own abode, He has reserved in everlasting chains under darkness for the judgment of the great day* (Jude 1:6 NKJV).

When the flood came in Genesis 7, this unnatural race called the Nephilim was wiped out along with all of humanity. The earth had become so wicked that God said that He regretted making man:

> *And the Lord was sorry that He had made man on the earth, and He was grieved in His heart* (Genesis 6:6 NKJV).

Noah was the only righteous man on earth, and scripture says that he was the only one who found grace in the eyes of the Lord. We know God saved Noah's family as well. If demons are in fact the spirits of the Nephilim, then they may be angry that they no longer have physical bodies. They want to be on the earth and so inhabit humans to continue their wickedness and destruction of the lives of God's people. Also, demons have superhuman strength, which would also bear witness that they could be the spirits of the Nephilim. Further understanding and the theory that the Nephilim are demonic spirits can be found in the book of Enoch. In this book, they are written about in greater detail along with apocalyptic writing that includes

the fall of the angels. While the book of Enoch is not part of canonical scripture, meaning it is not the inspired word of God through the Holy Spirit in the same way that Scripture is, it is still a well-known written text among Jews and referred to as a trusted ancient and historical writing.

The other viewpoint is that demons are the fallen angels that were kicked out of heaven along with Satan.

> *Now war arose in heaven, Michael and his angels fighting against the dragon. And the dragon and his angels fought back, but he was defeated, and there was no longer any place for them in heaven. And the great dragon was thrown down, that ancient serpent, who is called the devil and Satan, the deceiver of the whole world—he was thrown down to the earth, and his angels were thrown down with him* (Revelation 12:7-9 ESV).

I personally believe the fallen angels are more of the ruling hierarchy, the demonic princes of the unseen realm spoken about in the book of Daniel that I quoted earlier. Before the fall, this angelic army would have been mighty, noble, and beautiful. Rebellion changed that and altered the way they now appear; however, they still had the ability to oppose Michael and his angels.

> *And war broke out in heaven; Michael and his angels fought with the dragon; and the dragon and his angels fought, but they did not prevail, nor was a place found for them in heaven any longer* (Revelation 12:7-8 NKJV).

In my experience demons are stupid, childish, and whiney. They come out of people very easily when they are commanded to in Jesus' Name. They are used to being ordered around by the demonic hierarchy, and so when someone with authority speaks, they listen and obey. It's quite clear to me that demons don't carry much weight or authority outside of bossing one another around and deceiving people. There is no love lost between them; even though they are part of the same army, they are not loyal to one another and will do anything to survive in the person they are demonizing, even at the expense of getting another demon kicked out to secure their own survival! So, I lean more to the first theory of demons being the spirits of the Nephilim; however, this is not a theological debate as we have no definitive answer in the word of God.

Whatever you believe, it doesn't alter the fact that Satan's plan is to destroy and pervert mankind by using these lower-class spirit beings to enter people to carry out his plans of destruction. They are liars and thieves just like the father of lies, Satan himself. They are selfish, evil, perverted, grotesque-looking creatures. Fortunately for us, as they are supernatural beings, most of us cannot see their physical appearance. We do, however, see the manifestations of them acting out in people when they are being delivered.

The purpose of demons is to destroy and harass human beings. They work from the inside out. Each demon has its own evil characteristic. It could be anger, fear, guilt, selfishness, envy, jealousy, suicide, death, etc. It's these spirits or demons with their personalities and characteristics that enter a person. They remain if people allow those feelings, thoughts, emotions,

and behaviors to become habitual in their life. The demons take advantage of situations that involve traumas, abuses, violence, abandonment, accidents, death, suicide, panic, or shock. These are the doors that they enter through. You can recognize them in someone's life by the struggle that the person consistently lives in. The person will find it difficult trying to control their emotions or feelings in those areas. They are in a continual battle mentally, even though they have done everything they know to do as a believer to bring those thoughts into submission. Sometimes they can find it very difficult to keep focused or even think straight. The weight of heaviness and burden will just not shift. It's deep-seated, in the pit of the stomach, or blinding them in the mind. They are too embarrassed to tell the truth of how they are feeling and will say to people around them that everything is okay. It's not that they are intentionally misleading people. They don't know what it is themselves, mainly because they can still function, live a normal life, and love God. They hope or may believe things will get better someday, maybe during the next altar call! This is a classic picture of how demons operate in a person's life.

As I have said, demons are the lowest rank when it comes to the unseen realm; however, even within the lowest ranks of demons, there is a hierarchical system. There will always be a demon called the strongman present. This is the demon that gained entry first. He believes that the person he inhabits belongs to him and so takes authority over every other demon that enters. If you can discern the strongman and deal with him first, it makes it so much easier to expel or cast out every other demon. The strongman will be the dominant demon or main spirit operating. For example, if you were unwanted as a child, a spirit of rejection will be the first spirit to enter. As the first demon in or strongman, he will prop the door open for others to come in that are similar. Everything you do in your life will have a foundation of a fear of being rejected, which will affect every relationship you have and every job you do. Sometimes it will express itself as trying to be the best at everything and hating yourself if you don't meet impossible standards (that are set by you). Spirits of abandonment, loneliness, never being good enough, self-loathing, and self-harm will often be present.

Whenever we deal with a spirit of rejection, we also find a spirit of rebellion present. Rebellion will come with spirits of anger, hatred, wickedness, and unruliness. It makes the person rebel against every human authority and institution, especially a parent or guardian. The person will rebel because they want attention to appease the spirit of rejection that they cannot get rid of, and they will try everything to make themselves feel accepted by doing whatever they "feel" will make them accepted and loved. Again, it doesn't seem to make sense in the natural, but we are dealing with spirits here who cause emotions to rage in us. The truth is that it's the demons all along. They are impersonating and pretending to be us by taking over our personalities!

Likewise, when a strongman of depression is given a doorway into your life, it will attract spirits such as hopelessness, despair, suicide, self-harm, and death. You go from having fleeting moments of depression to them recurring on a regular basis. Because of this you start to lose hope and feel that you are never going to get better. When this happens, despair will enter your heart along with thoughts of suicide. Continuous thoughts of suicide many times will lead to self-harm and then thoughts of death will creep in with the deceptive voice that everyone would be better off without you. Can you see how demons work? They are very subtle, and they are very deceptive!

As a woman, if you have ever had an abortion, the guilt you may feel is overwhelming, but the strongman that enters first is a spirit of murder and death. I know that may seem extreme, but it's true because abortion is technically the murder of an unborn baby, the purposeful killing of a life. A spirit of murder will then wedge a door wide open in your life for the spirits or demons of guilt, shame, and depression. Whatever you do in life, you will always be brought back to or reminded of the decision you made. Anything that goes wrong in your life, you will associate it with the abortion. Demons of blame and even demons of sadness and regret will enter. You may even struggle to conceive again. In this case, many times we have had to call out the spirit of death that has hidden in a woman's womb!

As you are reading this, you may think, "Well, those emotions are natural, especially for a woman going through an abortion. Surely there will be regret, and of course there will be guilt or shame, especially if you were a Christian when you had an abortion." I just want to say this—there is a huge difference between conviction and condemnation. The Holy Spirit will convict us of any wrongdoing in our past or present that we need to deal with, He will help us confess or repent if needed, and He will do it with love and compassion so that we heal from the inside out. The sole purpose of demons is to destroy us from within, convincing us to condemn ourselves, convincing us we are bad and evil people who can never be forgiven or ever be good enough for God. Prolonged condemnation of anything we have done in our past or our present is demonic.

Demons work in packs. They know the more of them there are, the easier it will be to overwhelm the person they are demonizing, which is why a strongman will keep the door open for others to enter. They don't play fair, and their end game is to completely take over the person. People often ask me how many demons were cast out of them; my normal answer is that I couldn't keep count. On a side note, however, when it comes to deliverance, if you have the manpower to do it, I encourage you during the deliverance to have a scribe in the room, someone to take notes so that the person being set free can know what and how many demons were cast out of them. This helps them to remain free as they are aware of what types of demons will try to gain re-entry.

On average, the demons we cast out per person, I would say, would be between twenty to fifty, when they work in packs or clusters. (I know it sounds a lot!) However, sometimes each cluster will have a strongman, so it is little surprise that they all add up! This is one of the reasons why I wrote this book—to identify and expose the real enemy. The demons are convincing us that we are the ones messed up and that we can never match up to being the good Christian son or daughter God requires. I want to say, all those negative emotions and feelings are under the blood of Jesus, and if we are still feeling like that after salvation then there's only one place it is coming from! Remember, the old man/flesh died when we became born again. When we

got baptized in water it signified an outward demonstration of what had taken place in the inner man. We died to the flesh.

> *My old self has been crucified with Christ. It is no longer I who live, but Christ lives in me. So I live in this earthly body by trusting in the Son of God, who loved me and gave himself for me* (Galatians 2:20 NLT).

If Christ is in us, then everything from our old nature is gone!

> *Therefore, from now on, we regard no one according to the flesh. Even though we have known Christ according to the flesh, yet now we know Him thus no longer. Therefore, if anyone is in Christ, he is a new creation; old things have passed away; behold, all things have become new* (2 Corinthians 5:16-17 NKJV).

Demons are attention seekers and will take every opportunity they get to cause chaos on earth. They manipulate humans. While people in the world put demonic behavior down to personality traits or mental disorders or (in serious cases of wickedness) insanity, as believers we must be aware of what they are and what they do! When non-believers ask you the question, "If there's a God, why is there so much evil in the world?" point them to what you know, expose the enemy, let them know it's Satan and his demons that work in people to cause violence, abuse, evilness, and wars. Of course, people must cooperate and allow demons to work through them, but the reality is if Christians are only just understanding this, how do we expect people in the world to know this truth? If we don't tell them, they will

never know and will continue blaming God. When you know the truth, you are responsible to speak it out.

Wherever demons have come from and whatever your viewpoint regarding these wicked beings, demons for a while are here to stay. They will have their day in hell, don't worry, but that won't be until the final judgment. For now, as Christians, understanding their origin is informative, but understanding their purpose is vital in helping us deal with them. We have been given authority by Jesus Himself, but we must learn how to use it. I hope as you continue reading this book that the Holy Spirit will give you personal revelation and understanding of the authority you have over all demons and the part you play in destroying the works of darkness on earth.

CHAPTER 9

THE PRACTICAL PROCESS
OF DELIVERANCE
STEP BY STEP

S O, LET'S GET DOWN TO THE "NITTY GRITTY" OF DELIVER-
ance! What does it look like, how does it happen, and if I
recognize that I have demons, how do I get rid of them?

I am going to take you through this as practically as I can,
although there is a little more teaching here that's necessary for
understanding. At the end, there will be a prayer to pray if you
believe or recognize that you have demons. Freedom belongs to
you because that's what Christ died and rose again for!

I want to reiterate at this point—demons gain their entrance
in our lives through traumatic experiences, those experiences
that produced fear, guilt, shame, or terror in us. This is just a
small example of emotions.

In short, not everything is a demon! It's a natural part of
human emotion to have negative thoughts and feelings. We live
in a fallen world and there is so much to cause us concern. As
believers we know we have overcome the world because Jesus
said He has overcome the world and He lives on the inside
of us, but we can still fall foul of all the negative stuff that

surrounds us. Just because you have a sporadic emotion of anger, fear, guilt, anxiety, or stress does *not* mean you have a demon or that demons are on the inside of you. These types of emotions are natural to humans because of the fall, although as believers we can overcome them through the work of the Holy Spirit. It's important that I clarify this because I don't want any confusion about what being demonized looks like.

I just want to remind you again as a believer the areas you may be allowing Satan access into your life. Practicing sin as a Christian will open a door. So many Christians have one foot in the world and one foot in the church. Seriously, this is a dangerous place to be! You can cause more harm to yourself, your family, and your church by living this sort of life. Satan can manipulate you, influence you, and control you; he can also gain access to your finances. You become his puppet to destroy others who love the Lord. Sleeping around, getting drunk, watching pornography and practicing masturbation, purposely being dishonest, or knowingly walking in unforgiveness are all doors that will allow demons entry into your life. I'm not saying you don't love the Lord; you just may not fear Him if you are continually doing those things that He hates.

An area that most Christians are ignorant in is what you watch. Those things that you see or hear through your eye gate or ear gate and the negative atmospheres you surround yourself in will allow demons to enter, and if you allow this in your home, they will not just affect you but everyone living in your home. I heard an incredible message on "Atmospheres" by Pastor John Kilpatrick from the 1995 Brownsville Revival. He was explaining how lives were being radically changed during their nightly revival meetings, and specifically he was talking about marriages. Couples who hated one another beforehand, marriages that were on the brink of divorce, were being completely restored and delivered during the altar calls. The couples would often report that although during the services restoration would take place, the moment they arrived home, even pulling into the garage, their feelings of anger and frustration toward one another would return! They would then go back to the meetings, receive prayer, be restored once again, only to experience the same emotions when they returned home. There were so many stories like this that he went to prayer to ask the Holy Spirit what was happening.

Pastor John explained that they would regularly pray and clear the atmosphere in the sanctuary of any demons that they had cast out during altar calls and that they would invite the Holy Spirit to inhabit the place. He realized that this was the key! While in the revival, the atmosphere was full of faith, anointing, and God's presence because they had purposely invited Him to come and invade the space, but when these couples returned home, they were going back into the old atmosphere where arguments, anger, bitterness, and misunderstandings had reigned. He instructed every couple to cleanse the atmosphere in their home and to invite the Holy Spirit to reign in every room and in every area. When they did this, they reported that they had no more problems.

In the same message, Pastor John referred to how we invite demonic influences to enter our homes unchecked by what we allow to come through our television screens, our mobile phones, and our computers. He said our homes are like a platform in a railway station. The train comes along, the doors open, and whatever is on that train pours out into our home. The doors shut, the train leaves the station, but whatever got off that train stays in the home! An 18-rated movie, violence, adultery, lust, perversion, foul language. Our homes should be sanctuaries of peace where the Holy Spirit feels comfortable. They should not be comfortable dwellings for demons!

Another way we can become demonized is through any form of the occult, either practiced, watched, or entertained—it will always open a door! I believe most Christians recognize this and would not dream of practicing such things, but if you have ever been involved in the occult prior to being born again, then I would strongly encourage you that deliverance is needed, if you haven't already received it! I also wanted to mention it because the occult does not just involve Ouija boards, witches, divinations, spiritualists, or New Age! The dictionary definition says, "The occult is of or relating to magic, astrology, or any system claiming use or knowledge of secret or supernatural powers or agencies."

Doors are opened in our life when we are involved in anything outside of God that claims it has power to enhance our mind, body, or spirit. Meditation outside of God's word that encourages you to clear your mind or feel the energy on the inside of you is a form of the occult. Hypnosis where somebody else has access to control your mind for any period of time is a form of the occult. Practicing yoga, which has its roots in Hinduism and uses all the different positions of the "gods" to breathe and relax, is a form of the occult! Enneagram personality tests, reading predictions on social media like "Where will you be in five years' time?" all has its roots in fortune-telling, which is the occult!

How many of us click on those little games that pop up on our news feeds: "What does your name mean? Who will you marry? What does this year hold for you?" These things may sound harmless because in a way they are similar in nature to what we do as Christians. We meditate on His word by quietly praying and contemplating; we make vision boards, setting ourselves five-year goals! We must remember, however, that Satan takes God's truth and distorts it. He is able to deceive because he does it in a way that it is palatable even for the believer! So many Christians are involved in these kinds of practices, all of which originate in the occult.

I hope I haven't frightened you too much. Seriously, I have only mentioned a fraction of the occult practices many are unknowingly involved in! Sugarcoating what really happens in the spiritual realm isn't going to help anyone! Revealing how and why demons gain access to us as Christians is! Truth and truth alone sets the captives free. We are affected by what happens in the spiritual realm a million times more than what happens in the natural realm.

So practically, what does the process of deliverance look like? Well, it is generally the same for all those who make an appointment to come to our office. We prepare a private space at the church so we will not be interrupted or overheard (we always lock the doors). We have tissues, water, and a sick bucket, and we make sure we are prayed up as ministers, as we dare not even attempt to do anything without the assurance of the anointing and the presence of God. It doesn't mean we spend

hours in prayer before a deliverance, but it means we check in with the Holy Spirit to know and be assured of whose authority we are walking in and whose name we are using! We aim to have a team of at least three people. There will be one person who leads, and the others will support and speak in tongues quietly. We will always interact with one another. If one person hears from the Holy Spirit, we will allow that person to take the lead for a moment to call out the spirit, or they may just want to let the person leading know. Either way, the calling out of demons is done in an orderly fashion, calmly but forcibly and in unity.

There are five parts to a straightforward deliverance: counsel/talking, praying the prayer, breaking hereditary curses/bloodline ties, renouncing, and casting out. There are three things, however, that we require first from the person who is asking for deliverance. Number one, they must be honest—they cannot hide sins, hurts, or pain, past or present. We're bringing everything into the light. Satan is a legalist. He knows the word of God backward and forward, inside and out. If sins are hidden or you are too embarrassed to say what has happened to you, his demons are not going anywhere; they have a right to remain because the sin remains in the darkness.

Second, they cannot have unforgiveness in their heart toward anyone or anything. Satan knows the word and he knows if they won't forgive, he doesn't have to go anywhere, he can legally demonize them.

> *For if you forgive men their trespasses, your heavenly Father will also forgive you. But if you do not forgive men their trespasses, neither will your*

Father forgive your trespasses (Matthew 6:14-15 NKJV).

And whenever you stand praying, if you have anything against anyone, forgive him, that your Father in heaven may also forgive you your trespasses (Mark 11:25 NKJV).

Take heed to yourselves. If your brother sins against you, rebuke him; and if he repents, forgive him. And if he sins against you seven times in a day, and seven times in a day returns to you, saying, "I repent," you shall forgive him (Luke 17:3-4 NKJV).

Forgiveness may not always affect the person who has hurt you, but it will always affect you! When you forgive, you release all power that Satan has over your life. You shut the door in his face, giving God access to bless you. Forgiveness also allows God to intervene in the situation, whereas unforgiveness ties His hands! If you don't let go but hold that person to account yourself, God cannot do anything. This is why it is vital that people forgive when receiving deliverance.

Third is the most necessary thing—they must be desperate! They cannot have an attitude of "I'll give it a go and see what happens" or think "If it doesn't work, I'll try something else." Just like the woman with the issue of blood, they must be all in and so desperate to get free that they don't care what they look like or who sees them!

As I have mentioned in a previous chapter, I believe in counseling, and this is where it is used during deliverance. The first part is talking and investigating how doors were opened in the first place. Quite often within ten minutes we will identify

many of the root causes, the hows and the whys. It is often a shock to the person, yet at the same time the penny drops for them and for the first time in their lives they realize why they have been struggling with certain issues for so long. Everything all at once makes sense! I cannot overemphasize the importance of this part of the deliverance ministry, and even before we move to the second part, people begin to receive their deliverance.

> *Confess your trespasses to one another, and pray for one another, that you may be healed. The effective, fervent prayer of a righteous man avails much* (James 5:16 NKJV).

This process is all about bringing to the light what has been hidden. Satan has power because he's the hidden evil behind all sickness and disease. When we expose him or his schemes, he loses his power to control, and it's almost as if the demons lose their grip to hold on to a person. I describe it as the truth being like oil—the demons have nothing to hook their claws into any longer. When you confess sin or sins that have been committed against you, deliverance and healing immediately begin.

Once we have established all of this and the person is able to bring to light all that they can remember, we will move on to the prayer, which is the second part of the deliverance. The prayer covers several things that are necessary for deliverance. We use the same prayer that one of my favorite ministers on deliverance, Dr. Derek Prince, used. We ask the person to repeat the prayer audibly after one of us, line by line.

> *Lord Jesus Christ, I believe You died on the cross for my sins and rose again from the dead.*

You redeemed me by Your blood, and I belong to You,
and I want to live for You.
I confess all my sins, known and unknown.
I'm sorry for them all; I renounce them all.
I forgive all others as I want You to forgive me.
Forgive me now and cleanse me with Your blood.
I thank You for the blood of Jesus Christ, which
cleanses me now from all sin.
And I come to You now as my deliverer.
You know my needs, every spirit that binds, that
torments, that defiles.
That evil spirit, that unclean spirit.
I claim the promise of Your word:
Whosoever that calls on the Name of the Lord shall
be delivered.
I call upon You now.
In the Name of the Lord Jesus Christ, deliver me
and set me free.
Satan, I renounce you and all your works.
I loose myself from you in the Name of Jesus, and
I command you to leave me right now, in Jesus'
Name.
Amen.

There are several important points this prayer covers—the first is salvation, making sure the person is born again. If they're not, then we take this opportunity for them to receive Jesus into their hearts. Second, they forgive all others. As we've already discussed, the demons are not going anywhere unless there is forgiveness. Sometimes they find it very difficult to say this part, but we labor on it if we must and make them say the names of the people they need to forgive. Many times, they will say it through gritted teeth or with tears streaming down their faces, but you *must* make sure they say this part. I will often encourage a person that even if they don't feel like it, everything we do as believers is by faith anyway, and this is just something else they are doing by faith regardless of how they are feeling.

Third, they renounce the demons! This part is very powerful and even after the prayer we will get them to renounce emotions that have bound them (demonic spirits). The definition for the word *renounce* is "to repudiate; disown; to give up or put aside; to give up by formal declaration; to deny, disavow, discard, recant, cast off, divorce oneself from."

When the person being delivered renounces fear, guilt, shame, hatred, death, etc., we can then call those demons out because the person has vocally expressed that they no longer want them in their life or want to partner with them anymore! The demons must obey and leave.

After they have said the prayer, we will instruct them to stand up and open their mouth slightly. Demons only come out one way, and that's through the mouth because they are spirit beings, like breath. Sometimes we will explain the manner of manifestation in which the demons will come out; other times we will just stay quiet. It's not a part of everyday normal life for most people, and so we never want to make them feel nervous about what is about to happen. We just allow the Holy Spirit to lead us through it all from beginning to end, even guiding what we say or what we don't say.

The third part is when we break every hereditary curse coming down from their ancestors or through their blood-line. This again is a very important part of deliverance, which I addressed in the early part of the book. (Chapter 1—read again if you have forgotten!) At this point we also break any unhealthy soul ties, whether they be sexual, emotional, or phys-ical, again being led completely by the Holy Spirit.

The fourth part is where all the action generally happens, although many times at the point of breaking hereditary curses, the demons will start manifesting. We will have the person renounce all that they have spoken about, the things that have burdened them for years; it could be rejection, rebellion, addic-tion, hatred, idle words, abandonment, etc. Once they have done this, we will then make a statement like this:

> *Every demon attached to everything they have renounced, we command you to come out now in Jesus' Name, out now!*

Immediately, demons will start to manifest. Sometimes we will have to call them again and remind them that the person has renounced them and they can no longer stay. Demons hate to leave because it means they no longer have a body to use, which in turn means they cannot stay on the earth. They will try to hide, go quiet, or sometimes pretend they have gone! Through experience we are aware of all their tricks and know when they have really left.

There is always a mixture of manifestations. People may cough, retch, shout, contort, spin, crawl, jump, swing out, use expletive language, they may even burp demons out! Whatever

way, I never cease to be amazed; demons are like petulant children who hate being told what to do. It's almost as if they stamp their feet and whine—they will cry and pretend to be the person to avoid being expelled, they will even hide in a body part and the person being delivered will suddenly get a pain in that area. This is how we know where they are—the person may say, "My head is pounding," "My back is aching," or, "I can't move my fingers." We will just command them to leave or sometimes we will touch that area and almost immediately they move and come out. Some deliverance ministers prefer not to touch those being delivered; for us, we find this very effective when led by the Holy Spirit.

Demons will even make the person fall asleep by pretending they are free and are just resting. When they really don't want to go, they will try to argue their case, why they should stay. For me personally, I don't engage in much conversation with demons. On occasion I will question the demon if the situation requires it, but demons are liars, so much of what they say is nonsense anyway. The normal verbiage from a demon is, "No, I won't leave," "She is mine," "I'm going to kill him." Sometimes they cackle and laugh in your face, mocking you. I will always close this stuff down straightaway and take control. If I am feeling particularly annoyed with the demon, I may tell it to shut up and get out. Normally, I will give instructions, especially when the demons won't allow the person to open their mouths. I will say something like, "Allow him to speak," or if they are rolling all over the floor and being particularly demonstrative, I will say, "Stop now and get up!" This may all sound a little strange, and at first it was weird interacting with these evil spirits in this way, but when you recognize where they come from and the evil and misery they cause people, you understand why Jesus instructed us to do this. We are literally carrying out His command, which He has anointed us to do!

I will talk in the next chapter about what happens after someone has been delivered, but right now I want to give you instruction on self-deliverance. If you recognize that you personally need deliverance, you can do one of two things—you can make an appointment and ask a minister who is familiar with casting out demons to pray for you, or you can deal with it right now! I will say, having someone else pray for you initially is the best course of action (plus it reduces any probability that you have pride in your heart), but it is good to start the process off and deal with things the moment you recognize you have demons.

It's four simple steps.

The first step is to ask the Holy Spirit to reveal to you those doors that were opened in your life, giving access to the demons. Ask Him to give you discernment to know what demons they are. Once you have this information, then the second step is to pray the prayer. The third step is to renounce them. Remember, these are deep emotional struggles that you feel in the pit of your stomach, the emotions or addictions that continually harass you.

Renounce the demons, addressing them directly, and command them to go in Jesus' Name. Then, step four, you start to exhale and breathe them out. You may feel weird in your stomach or throat; you may start coughing or spitting up phlegm.

Whatever happens, don't get freaked out! Demons go out in all manner of ways.

Let me give you this example so that you know you are doing it correctly. If the Holy Spirit has revealed to you that it is a spirit of self-hatred, insecurity, low self-esteem, then you would say something like this:

> *I renounce the spirit of self-hatred, of insecurity and low self-esteem, and in the Name of Jesus I command each one of you to leave me now! Out in Jesus' Name!*

Then start to blow out.

You may need to repeat this process several times. You should have a lighter feeling on the inside of you as if a heavy weight has been lifted off your chest, shoulders, head, or out of your stomach area. You should also be able to think a lot more clearly! Now take a moment to spend with the Holy Spirit, ask Him to fill you afresh, start to worship, and give God thanks for His goodness.

CHAPTER 10

KEEPING THE
HOUSE CLEAN
**WHAT SHOULD
I DO AFTER
DELIVERANCE?**

O NE THING I HAVE LEARNED AS I HAVE BECOME MORE
experienced in the deliverance ministry is that it's not
always a one-time deal! When I first started delivering people,
I expected it to be the ultimate answer, that it would solve all
their problems! In fact, deliverance is an answer. It's not the
only answer, but it is the missing key for many to live an abundant life. Deliverance is the start of a whole new walk with the
Lord—a walk of freedom, a walk of understanding, and new
vision. It's the most amazing revelation you can receive outside
of salvation, but it must be maintained. To know and understand true freedom is the most incredible thing.

I also think the realization of how Satan uses demons to
attack people and that he will stop at nothing to destroy God's
creation is such a revelation in the spiritual realm that people
quite often look back on their past lives with disbelief knowing that it was Satan that had bound them all along. To know

and understand how demons have controlled you and decisions you may have made in your past life makes you mad that you allowed it, but it also makes you want to shout it from the rooftops to tell other people that they too can experience this type of freedom!

Deliverance is a huge step because it demands vulnerability, honesty, and openness. I applaud anyone who will open their life up to receive it. It is the best step you could take, and I would never make any apology for operating in this ministry. The world *and* the church need it more than they know!

Keeping the house clean once you have received deliverance is not just a suggestion, it is a necessity. It's interesting because after deliverance, without exception, approximately three days later those demons that were cast out will come knocking on the door again! (Although in one case we encountered, they came knocking within the hour!) People will report that they have had a couple of great days worshiping and spending time in the word, filling up their "house," feeling lighter, seeing more clearly, but then suddenly out of the blue, they feel like those demons have come back again. Sometimes they will say it's even worse! I tell them immediately—the demons are now on the outside of them, but they are making the biggest noise hoping you will let them back in!

Our bodies are described in God's word as both temples and houses! When demons are cast out of our houses, we must lock all the doors and windows. We do this by filling up the empty space (which is what it feels like on the inside once demons have been expelled) with worship, the word, and the Holy Spirit. Demons are frustrated because they have been kicked out of "their" home, so they will shake the doors, rattle the windows, bang and crash, and make all kinds of noises so you will pay them attention and open the door. The only way for them to gain entry is for you to start entertaining that emotion or addiction again, and if you believe incorrectly that the demons never left you in the first place, they will gain access all over again. They are *not* on the inside because they have been cast out; they just lie to you to convince you they are.

> *When an unclean spirit goes out of a man, he goes through dry places, seeking rest, and finds none. Then he says, "I will return to my house from which I came." And when he comes, he finds it empty, swept, and put in order. Then he goes and takes with him seven other spirits more wicked than himself, and they enter and dwell there; and the last state of that man is worse than the first. So shall it also be with this wicked generation* (Matthew 12:43-45 NKJV).

This scripture has a double meaning about what is coming in the last days, but in our context we understand it as it refers to a house that is cleansed and clean from demons with everything back in its rightful place but is left unlocked! If the doors are not locked by filling up with the word, worship, and the Holy Spirit, the demon or strongman will return and bring even worse demons with it than the first time around.

We always instruct people how to deal with the demons when they try to regain entry. They must be rebuked and reminded that they are no longer welcome and that they have been cast out once and for all. We instruct people to worship, give thanks, and praise God for their freedom. We encourage them to speak the word out loud, declaring their newly found freedom.

Many times, people will come back for more deliverance. Those who have been involved in the occult, abused, or who have been in addictions are the most likely to come back. The demons have generally been in them for a long time, and they are a lot in number. Sometimes also God will choose to deliver people gradually because He knows they wouldn't be able to cope with everything all at once. I probably haven't mentioned this before, but delivering someone can be quite the workout for you and for them. Demons can get physical, so you must have your wits about you, but those receiving deliverance will often say they feel like they have gone ten rounds with Mike Tyson! I think most times that we have delivered those who needed deliverance more than once, they have eventually received complete freedom by the third or fourth time. They will come once a week or once a fortnight. These are genuine, born-again believers who love God and who live godly lifestyles. Some come back after a long period of time but again are genuine in their need for more deliverance.

Our associate pastor, who I wrote about in Chapter 2, after two years received more deliverance! Once you have had any form of deliverance, you can tell when the heaviness either comes back or something new appears. She knew straight-away, and although it wasn't a planned deliverance (it was in the middle of a church conference!), she got free! We laugh so hard about it now because she was very loud! Our prayer team surrounded her immediately, and a few of us got on our knees because she had fallen to the floor. We started calling those things out. What was so amazing was that one of our tall, African brothers in the church started worshiping over us, and the wingspan of his arms stretched right out, covering us all completely. He literally looked like an angel, and even though it was loud and those demons coming out of her were angry, it was the most beautiful thing to be a part of. The presence of God and the anointing would not allow those demons to stay on the inside of her.

Talking afterward, she had recognized that there was a point since she had been free when she had allowed some negative and angry thinking to take a hold of her. Left unchallenged and without resistance, those demons took that smallest of opportunities and entered her like a shot! It was the heaviness that weighed her down that made her realize exactly what was going on. Seeing someone get free is the best part of deliverance. It makes you smile and give thanks! You never get familiar with the feeling of being a part of something so wild, wonderful, and supernatural!

Keeping your house clean continually in the spirit is the same as keeping your house clean in the natural! It must be done consistently and regularly with some areas needing to be deep cleaned once a year. We all know you can't clean your house from top to bottom once and expect it to stay clean for the rest of your life. There are areas that need extra work that you must pay special attention to. Again, it's the same with our spiritual house—when there are areas that have caused us problems in the past, we must make sure it is being taken care of, that we are applying the word to that area, and that we are

watching and being mindful that it needs protecting. Satan will always attack our weak areas; he has his demons wait and look for the opportune moment to slip back in, but if we keep our house clean, he will have no opportunity!

If you don't realize the importance of maintaining a clean house once you have received deliverance or struggle to understand why you need to, there may be other issues going on like this next story I want to share. There are many people who ask for deliverance that treat it like a fix, just the same as if they were on drugs. The first time they receive it, they are amazed and feel wonderful. We give them all the usual counsel afterward about keeping their house clean and filling up on the word, worship, and presence of God and warning them of the dangers if they don't do this. They agree to all we are saying in the moment, but within days or weeks they return asking for more deliverance because they didn't do anything we instructed them to do, and they messed up!

When I first started operating in this ministry, I didn't realize that this would happen, and I thought it was something I was doing wrong! I soon learned that like anything else God instructs us to do, you still must live a holy life before Him, and as a believer you can't be living an ungodly lifestyle and expect the word or deliverance to work for you.

We had one person who came for the first time several years ago, and it honestly sounded like a legion had come out! As we were delivering them in one part of the church, some of our staff members could hear the noise through the ceiling and thought it sounded like a huge crowd of men screaming and shouting. Afterward, the person felt as we expected them to feel—lighter in body and mind—and even though we knew they would need some counseling for their onward journey as a Christian, we believed they got free. I was so disappointed when they contacted us within days to say the same spirits we cast out were still attacking them. It didn't make sense to me at first because I was sure we had dealt with the demons they were describing. In my mind, I was thinking, *What on earth did we cast out then?*

They made another appointment, and a week later they came in. The deliverance went much the same way as the first time, with the same sounds of a growling dog coming out of their mouth and the same manifestations—retching and bending over spitting phlegm everywhere. They said they felt free, and I was glad it was over. I could hardly believe my eyes when they came to the altar for ministry on the following Sunday morning for more deliverance! A few of our team prayed, and just like the previous two times they started shouting and growling. It was loud and demonstrative and drawing much attention. All of us involved in the deliverance just looked at each other with the same expression on our faces. I would say it was a perplexed look rather than confusion, but we all questioned what was taking place.

One thing I know, and I say it all the time when we find ourselves in situations like this—there is nothing wrong with the Name of Jesus, His blood, or His word. There is nothing wrong with the confidence we have in our authority to cast demons out, so it must be something to do with the person we are delivering. I shut the whole thing down pretty quickly because of the distraction it was causing at the altar. I told them to come into the office during the week so we could discuss what was happening. When they came in, they repeated the same thing—that the demons we had cast out were still there and still attacking them. When we got down to the truth of the matter, however, what they didn't reveal before their first deliverance was that they were living immorally with their partner and that they were still sporadically taking drugs. I was far from impressed and was annoyed because they should have known better and at least shared this information the first time we sat down with them. We decided not to deliver them again until they had changed their lifestyle and stopped taking drugs.

If people are not living right according to the word of God, demons are able to regain access after they have been delivered. The whole point is that we keep our house clean; it does not mean we cannot make a mistake, but it does mean we cannot live a life that we know God cannot bless. Sex outside of marriage, addictions to pornography, taking drugs, smoking, drinking alcohol to get drunk—these things make your house very unholy, very unclean, and demons love uncleanness.

When we recognize the evil surrounding us and the world we live in, it takes the most dedicated Christian not to be affected by any of it. None of us intentionally sin or do things on purpose to displease God, but quite often unknowingly we can allow a demon to take a hold of us. It could be in areas of family issues, church offenses, the friendships we keep; even as leaders we are subject to ignorantly opening doors! Let me encourage you, deal with any overwhelming emotion or feeling immediately. Do not let it fester and do not meditate on it. As the word instructs us, we must cast down vain imaginations and anything that sets itself up against God and His truth. If you make it a priority to always clean your spiritual house with the word of God, demons will not be able to gain a foothold or take advantage or enter your life.

I just want to finish this chapter with some keys that I believe will help you to stay free.

- Be filled with the Holy Spirit.
- Become rooted in His word.
- Close every door that was open.
- Get rid of anything and everything that once connected you to those demons (alcohol, websites for pornography, unhealthy relationships).
- Attend church and become active.
- Have an accountability or prayer partner.
- Do not purposely sin.

Keep your house clean!

CHAPTER 11

DELIVERANCE AND HEALING
CONNECTING THE DOTS

When evening had come, they brought to Him many who were demon-possessed. And He cast out the spirits with a word, and healed all who were sick, that it might be fulfilled which was spoken by Isaiah the prophet, saying: "He himself took our infirmities and bore out sicknesses."

—MATTHEW 8:16-17 NKJV

And Jesus went about all Galilee, teaching in their synagogues, preaching the gospel of the kingdom, and healing all kinds of sickness and all kinds of disease among the people. Then His fame went throughout all Syria; and they brought to Him all sick people who were afflicted with various diseases and torments, and those who were demon-possessed, epileptics, and paralytics; and He healed them.

—MATTHEW 4:23-24 NKJV

WOMAN, THOU ART LOOSED. WE HAVE ALL HEARD THIS statement being made. It is from the scripture found in the book of Luke. You may have thought that it's just connected to the woman being physically healed and it is about physical healing, but it is so much more than that too. This passage of scripture gives us a clear insight into the connection between healing and deliverance.

It was on a Sabbath and Jesus was teaching in the synagogue; the word says that He noticed the woman bent over.

> *Now He was teaching in one of the synagogues on the Sabbath. And behold, there was a woman who had a spirit of infirmity eighteen years, and was bent over and could in no way raise herself up. But when Jesus saw her, He called her to Him and said to her, "Woman, you are loosed from your infirmity." And He laid His hands on her, and immediately she was made straight, and glorified God* (Luke 13:10-13 NKJV).

First, I love the fact that Jesus noticed *her!* I should imagine the synagogue was packed full of people because Jesus was in town teaching the scriptures, and everyone was eager to hear what He had to say, yet in among everyone, He noticed her. I believe it was a mixture of His love and compassion that moved Him to speak to her. She didn't even ask to be healed; along with all the others, she probably just wanted to hear Jesus speak. This woman was so used to living with her condition, she may not have wanted to cause a distraction or disturb the Teacher. I just love the fact that it was Jesus who made the first move.

We can gain so much understanding about healing and deliverance from this whole passage. This woman was bent over. Jesus knew it was a spirit that was causing her to be bent over and not a deformity, and He called it out straightaway. He said, "Be loosed." He knew exactly what He was dealing with. A spirit had been restricting her movement for eighteen years. She couldn't even look up to see His face. If it had been a physical illness, then Jesus would have spoken directly to the back or spine of the lady and commanded it to straighten up, like in many other cases in the New Testament when He either spoke directly to the person or spoke to the sickness.

I need to say here that all sickness and disease has its roots in the demonic, but not all illnesses or sickness and disease we suffer is a demon. There are numerous ways our physical bodies are affected in this fallen world. Illness can be hereditary; it may be because of a dysfunctional organ in our body, a deficiency in a chromosome or gene, or a deficiency in the womb. We could catch a disease or virus or be the one spreading it to another person. We could be involved in an accident and break or damage our bodies. Many of us have suffered in one or more ways like this; however, there are also direct demonic attacks aimed at us that bring sickness and disease, and it's only in the Name of Jesus that we can be free from this type of sickness and be healed. The woman who was loosed was one of those.

We can tell it was demonic because if it had been a physical illness, He may have said something along the lines of, "I command your back or spine to be healed," but He didn't even acknowledge the fact that she was bent over or the issue was with her back. Neither did He have a conversation with

a demon, nor did a demon manifest in front of Him, but He knew immediately through discernment that this lady's illness was caused by a demonic spirit. He ignored the demon but spoke to what the demon was doing, which was physically binding her and preventing her from standing upright. The moment He commanded the woman to be loosed, the spirit of infirmity left, Jesus laid hands on her, and for the first time in eighteen years she was able to stand up straight and look someone directly in the eyes. How awesome was it that it was Jesus' eyes she gazed into first? Can you imagine the emotion of that moment? We can read it in the following translations:

> *And there was a woman who for eighteen years had had a sickness caused by a spirit; and she was bent double, and could not straighten up at all* (Luke 13:11 NASB).
>
> *He saw a woman who had been crippled by an evil spirit. She had been bent double for eighteen years and was unable to stand up straight* (Luke 13:11 NLT).

The spirit of infirmity had no choice but to leave. Jesus didn't give it an option. That demon must have been so mad that after eighteen years it had been evicted! It had gone unseen for all those years because everyone, including the woman, believed it was just a natural sickness that she was suffering. Praise God the Father sent Jesus! He came to destroy all the works of darkness and to heal all those who were and are oppressed of the devil. He revealed so much truth through this situation that those who thought they knew everything about God were embarrassed!

All the eyes of the people were on Jesus, including the religious leaders, because it was the Sabbath and, once again, He had healed someone. Jesus was annoyed with them already because they questioned and challenged everything He did. We can read in Mark 3:1-6 of the account of the man with the withered hand that Jesus had healed on a Sabbath. Jesus was angry with the religious leaders because of the hardness of their hearts. It grieved Him so much that they didn't care about the suffering of the people and were not loving them and taking care of them as they were supposed to—they just cared about their appearance and everyone fearing them because they loved their positions! When Jesus laid hands on this woman and healed her, He not only set her free, but He exposed the heart of their religious mindsets for everyone to see and hear!

> *But the ruler of the synagogue answered with indignation, because Jesus had healed on the Sabbath; and he said to the crowd, "There are six days on which men ought to work; therefore come and be healed on them, and not on the Sabbath day."*
>
> *The Lord then answered him and said, "Hypocrite! Does not each one of you on the Sabbath loose his ox or donkey from the stall, and lead it away to water it? So ought not this woman, being a daughter of Abraham, whom Satan has bound—think of it— for eighteen years, be loosed from this bond on the Sabbath?" And when He said these things, all His adversaries were put to shame; and all the multitude rejoiced for all the glorious things that were done by Him* (Luke 13:14-17 NKJV).

While they were busy getting all mad that Jesus broke one of the laws, Jesus was more interested in freeing and healing this woman who hadn't been able to function properly for eighteen years! Not only that, but she was a daughter of Abraham, part of God's holy people, the people of promise, whom Satan had snared for years and whom Jesus had come to set free. It was so evident that the religious leaders didn't care about the people. They were more concerned with trying to discredit Jesus and all the miracles that He was performing. They were determined to call Him out because He made them look so bad in front of all the people.

On this occasion, their plotting against Him backfired, a religious spirit was exposed in the heart of the ruler of the synagogue, and it wasn't just him being put to shame. The scripture says all of Jesus' adversaries were put to shame. Jesus didn't mince His words. He called them out for what they were—*hypocrites* enjoying their position of being the holy men. Their appearance meant more to them than seeing God's people healed and whole. Miracles speak for themselves; they don't need to be explained. The people witnessed it with their very own eyes. Once this lady was bound, and now she was free. That's all that mattered to the crowd!

We must never allow ourselves, regardless of the circumstances or situation, to become religious about how, why, when, or where we should pray for someone to receive healing! Wherever the need is, we should be praying. We can get overly consumed with the "right" way to pray for people. Where is the appropriate place, or what we should say? Who should we be asking, Jesus or the Holy Spirit? Should we anoint them? Is it

the prayer of faith we should be declaring? Should we be saved forever to even qualify to pray for the sick? The whole reason Jesus healed people was so they would know how much they were loved by the Father, which in turn brought glory to the Father's Name. Jesus reached out to the woman because He was incensed that she was a daughter of Israel suffering needlessly. Jesus didn't care what the religious people thought, if He was praying how they prayed, or if He was saying the right things. It was about freeing the people who needed His help! He prayed for people when He was moved with compassion, He prayed with people who had faith, and He prayed for people who asked Him.

Through this specific story we can see the connection between deliverance and healing. It was a spirit that had caused sickness in her body for eighteen years. Demons not only affect our emotional state, but they also affect our physical state. The most common spirit that causes sickness, as in this case, is the spirit of infirmity. This spirit is responsible mainly for three types of sickness—those that the doctors cannot diagnose, those that are terminal, or those for which there is no treatment available. The spirit will bind a part of the body, preventing it from functioning correctly. It will also cause illness in specific areas, targeting them on purpose.

Many times, when we are praying for healing over someone's body, we will bind the spirit of infirmity first. Once that spirit is bound, healing starts to flow. That's why Jesus first said, "Woman, thou are loosed from thine infirmity." He knew she had been bound by Satan and instantly broke the hold Satan had over her. Notice the scripture says He then laid hands on

her, and she stood upright. He loosed her from that spirit first, and then she was able to receive her healing.

Again, we can read in Matthew 12:22 (NLT):

> *Then a demon-possessed man, who was blind and couldn't speak, was brought to Jesus. He healed the man so that he could both speak and see.*

It couldn't be clearer that it was a demon preventing this man from speaking and seeing! I find it so interesting that the people who had the biggest problem with Jesus casting out demons and setting the people free were the religious leaders. This time they accused Jesus of working for Satan, but Jesus, already knowing their thoughts that they were jealous of the authority He walked in, dealt instantly with their ignorant attitudes.

> *But when the Pharisees heard about the miracle, they said, "No wonder he can cast out demons. He gets his power from Satan, the prince of demons."*
> *Jesus knew their thoughts and replied, "Any kingdom divided by civil war is doomed. A town or family splintered by feuding will fall apart. And if Satan is casting out Satan, he is divided and fighting against himself. His own kingdom will not survive. And if I am empowered by Satan, what about your own exorcists? They cast out demons, too, so they will condemn you for what you have said"*
> (Matthew 12:24-27 NLT).

I love the fact that He picked up on this. Before Jesus, the only people able to cast out demons were the rabbis, but they

were not able to do it with the authority Jesus did, and they were nowhere near as effective as Him. That's why the people were amazed by Jesus—because of the way the evil spirits obeyed His every word. With one word He was able to cast the demons out. He continued to correct and rebuke the Pharisees:

> *But if I am casting out demons by the Spirit of God, then the Kingdom of God has arrived among you. For who is powerful enough to enter the house of a strong man [like Satan] and plunder his goods? Only someone even stronger—someone who could tie him up and then plunder his house* (Matthew 12:28-29 NLT).

He makes the statement here that the very fact that He can cast out demons and heal people the way He does is proof that He is operating by the Spirit of God and that He has the authority of the Kingdom of God. Sadly, they were so blinded by their jealousy that they couldn't see what or who was standing in front of them. We, too, have that same authority because we have the spirit of God, and we represent His Kingdom.

There's another passage of scripture that links the healing of evil spirits and infirmities:

> *And certain women who had been healed of evil spirits and infirmities—Mary called Magdalene, out of whom had come seven demons, and Joanna the wife of Chuza, Herod's steward, and Susanna, and many others who provided for Him from their substance* (Luke 8:2-3 NKJV).

Luke is referring to Jesus traveling through different villages with His twelve disciples. He mentions various women with whom we are familiar who were healed from demonic spirits and sickness and who then went on to support Jesus financially and practically in His ministry. Here again, we can see that Luke references the words "healed from evil spirits" and "infirmities" in the same sentence. The dictionary defines the word *infirmity* as "an affliction, debilitation, disorder, sickliness." We know an evil spirit is a demon that can cause those same issues in our bodies. They can afflict us with pain and suffering; we become debilitated in certain areas, preventing us from functioning the way we were designed to. Then because of the sickness we are experiencing, it causes all manner of disorder in our lives, and we may end up becoming sick in other areas of our body! I believe it is clear that a spirit of infirmity is a demon, and when that spirit gains access to us, its primary goal is to bind our physical bodies so we are impeded in the call of God on our lives.

It's important when we are praying for the sick that we ask the Holy Spirit first how we should pray for the person! Jesus was so in tune with the Holy Spirit that He knew exactly how to deal with the woman bent over. We cannot just pray from what we know or what we think we should be praying or because it's what we usually do. Every person is different, and the Holy Spirit will instruct us accordingly. Like I said, not every sickness is a demon, but because we know some sicknesses *are* caused by demons, we need to know which is what and how we should pray!

To do this, it's imperative that we operate in the gift of discernment. It's one of the most important gifts that the Holy

Spirit has given us when it comes to praying for people. As we know, the spirit of discernment is one of the nine gifts of the Spirit, and it's not just given to us so that we can discern what is right and wrong. The scripture actually says it's the discerning of spirits, meaning discernment gives us supernatural insight into what spirit is operating in a person's life, whether it's a good spirit or a bad spirit. And let me just make this statement here—the only good spirit is the Holy Spirit, so if it's not Him then it's not a good spirit! This is what enables the Christian to know what to say and how to pray for the sick.

Before having revelation of this, I can remember that on several occasions I would pray for the sick and be so frustrated that nothing would happen. I would pray without consulting the Holy Spirit or asking for the gift of discernment. I would pray in the hope that the person I was praying for would feel at least a small improvement in their body! I would use that famous scripture about the lepers being healed as they "went" to get me off the hook when no improvement was felt or experienced in the moment. I would quote this scripture and then pray again and thank God that they would start to see healing in the next day or two.

Please hear me, I know that this can and does happen, but when you quote it without hearing the Holy Spirit telling you that's the case, using it as a reason to justify why they haven't been healed is not good! Jesus' power to heal is as real today as when He walked the earth. He also said we would do greater works than He did. We always question why some people are healed and others are not, but when you have a spirit of discernment, you will not only know how to pray, but you will also be

able to discern whether you need to deal with a spirit of infirmity first or if you can just pray the prayer of faith from James 5. Knowing how to pray means you either address the spirit or you believe by faith in the healing power of the Holy Spirit and deal directly with the sickness. This is something we all need to know. Honestly, if we prayed this way, we would see a lot more people healed. Jesus' power has not waned throughout time. It's as strong and potent today as it ever was, we just need to learn to listen to the Holy Spirit.

I have seen hundreds of people healed in 40-plus years of being a Christian, and I have personally laid my hands on many people and witnessed them receiving their healing. In the same breath, I can also say that I have witnessed many not being healed. However, I gladly am also able to say that since I have been involved in the ministry of deliverance, the number of people receiving their healing and the ones I have personally laid hands on who have been healed has super exceeded anything that has gone before! My approach is no longer with any feeling of trepidation, but it is with boldness and an assurance that when I pray for them, they will be healed. I don't expect anything less. If, for some reason, healing doesn't manifest, I don't look inward for the "failure" of the "task" and blame myself for my lack of faith, and I don't switch the tables on them and blame them for having no faith. Obviously, you must have faith, whether it's you, them, or both of you. Faith is needed in the mix; there's no other way to witness a miracle. But if nothing happens, it's not my "go to" anymore. I recognize that there could be other forces at work suppressing or preventing the healing we expect to flow in that person's body. I love the scripture in Psalm 107:20 (NKJV):

> *He sent His word and healed them, and delivered*
> *them from their destructions.*

His word works. He sends the word to us to bring healing, and whether that's speaking the word of faith or casting out a demon, the instructions are all found in His word. However, there is one thing we know that will prevent healing from flowing. I am powerless to do anything if the person I am praying for has unforgiveness in their heart. I can categorically tell you that if this is the case, the person will not get healed. Satan has the upper hand, and no amount of faith or casting out a devil will work if the person is nurturing offense or unforgiveness. Getting rid of offense and unforgiveness is key when we are delivering people, and it's the same when you are praying for someone to receive healing. Demons love it when we hold offense or unforgiveness in our heart because they know they can keep us bound in sickness unhindered! If this is the case and you discern it's the problem when praying for someone, then you must simply ask the person to confess the sin of unforgiveness. If they are genuine in their repentance, continue praying for them and expect the healing to take place.

Having an understanding that all sickness has its roots in the demonic is the first step in knowing that everyone you lay hands on can be healed. Jesus overcame *all* the powers of the enemy, and so if the devil is restricting, binding, or afflicting people in any way, we can rebuke him, bind him, or cast out whatever spirit is operating. I have experienced this repeatedly,

especially when those who come for deliverance also have sickness in their body. One lady who had been ill through neglect since she was a child came for deliverance. She had lots of other things going on in her life, but her illness had restricted her for years. It was an ulcerative colitis that caused much bleeding. It was getting worse as she got older, to the point that it had become so severe that she was due to have a feeding tube fitted. When we cast out the other demons that were oppressing her, we discerned that it was a spirit of infirmity that was binding her physically. We called it out and she was not only delivered from the demons in her soul, but she was also set free and delivered from the spirit of infirmity binding her physical body. Her doctor was amazed that there was such a dramatic improvement and reported that no feeding tube would be needed. As of today, she is still symptom-free. I can't deny the facts—this has happened over and over during deliverance, even to the point of wombs being healed.

When women have suffered repeated miscarriages in their bodies with no reasonable medical explanation, we are always aware it may involve a spirit of some kind. Again, this is where we completely rely on the Holy Spirit for discernment. In the past, when praying for women, we have called out the spirit of death, a thieving spirit, even a spirit of grief connected to the womb. Sometimes, in the case of women who have had an abortion, it is the spirit of murder as well as the spirit of death that we have had to cast out. This is because an abortion is a termination or destruction of a life, and knowingly or not, a murder has been committed. I know this sounds dramatic, but demons don't play. They take every opportunity or doorway that has been opened to them to inhabit a person, and abortion is a wide-open door!

Demons will make use of any spiritual legal right they can find. Unconfessed murder is sin. When this sin has taken place, a demon is able to enter the soul. Whether a woman has been forced to have an abortion or did it thinking it was the right thing to do, it is murder, and a demon will take advantage of this opportunity to enter. Why am I mentioning this? Well, the reason it is important when it comes to healing is because demons inhabit body parts. They will cause debilitation in an area, creating death, destruction, and pain to that area of the body. A womb is created to nurture and produce life. What better way for Satan to destroy a woman than to steal from her the very thing that uniquely belongs to her—the ability to nurture life. I mean, that is a whole other book, right? But concerning this subject, it's where a demon can take authority if the abortion has never been repented of or, in the case of deliverance, if it is not renounced. The moment the woman does this, we get the pleasure in casting out every one of those demons from her womb. They lose their right to stay, and healing can be received!

I will repeat myself—this is why being led by the Holy Spirit is the ultimate key when we are praying for healing. He will lead you into what you should say and how you should pray, and He will give you a word of knowledge or discernment if a person has unforgiveness in their heart.

Since I have been involved in the deliverance ministry, as I've already said, the boldness I have had in praying for the sick has grown exponentially. I've always known what the word says regarding how we need to use our faith when it comes to praying for the sick, and throughout my Christian journey I've mainly thought that faith was the only ingredient needed to see miracles take place. Through much experience, I can say that both faith and deliverance are tools given and provided to ensure complete healing for us all. I believe what I have mentioned here are keys to seeing people healed.

I can't recall anyone in the Bible who did not receive their healing when they asked for it. I think the problem we have as Christians when it comes to praying for the sick (and something I have admitted to being guilty of myself) is the sin of presumption. It's the same sin that prevented Moses from receiving his promise in full, and I believe some of us are still falling into the same trap today. If we have prayed for someone in a certain way before and they were healed, we try the same way again on the next person! We all know Moses' story. He was guilty of doing this exact thing, presumption, and it got him into a lot of trouble. It's because along with presumption comes pride. Moses thought he knew what he should do without feeling the need to consult with God. It was the key that unlocked the miracle of water coming out of the rock the first time, so why not use it again? We do it all the time, and I'm sure it's a frustration to the Holy Spirit who is always waiting for us to consult Him as to how we need to pray for each individual.

Even though I've said that we should avoid following formulas when it comes to healing because each person is different (this is true!), there is an order we can follow that will help us pinpoint and direct our prayer quickly. Whenever you stand in front of someone ready to pray for their healing, first thank

God for His anointing on you that brings the empowerment of the Holy Spirit to heal. It breaks every yoke of bondage, including demonic bondage. Ask the person what they need prayer for, even if it's obvious to you. Their expectation is key to the anointing flowing and them receiving their healing. Asking for prayer is admitting you need God's help; it's part of walking in humility. If the Holy Spirit is not instructing you in a specific way, then pray the prayer of faith as instructed in the word.

> *And the prayer of faith will save the sick, and the Lord will raise him up. And if he has committed sins, he will be forgiven* (James 5:15 NKJV).

This means knowing that Jesus made a way for us to be healed by taking on every form of sin, sickness, disease, and death on His body at the cross. It means by the laying on of your hands on the person you are expecting and believing by faith that the sickness the person is suffering will have no power or authority to stay on their body because of the sacrifice Jesus made. You then use His name that is above all things named in heaven, on earth, and under the earth, which He has given us to declare that they are healed (Philippians 2:9-10). If the Holy Spirit tells you to address the injury, illness, or pain directly by laying hands upon the area affected, do it. If it is demonic and it's a spirit of infirmity, then you will first need to rebuke the spirit, cast it out, and then command the body part to be healed in Jesus' Name. Use your faith, boldness, and the authority you have in Jesus' Name to see the sick person become well. Refuse to be intimidated by what's in front of you but be moved by love and compassion to see the person made whole.

Deliverance is healing; healing is deliverance. They are so closely related when it comes to both physical and emotional ailments. Our bodies are uniquely designed and created by God. When one part of us is affected, our whole body can experience both the physical and emotional symptoms. The Holy Spirit is our teacher, our guide, our power source, and whatever we must deal with, whoever we need to pray for, He is the One who has the answers.

I should imagine some of you reading this will already have revelation and understanding of how to pray for the sick and you may have been doing it for years, but I felt it necessary to write this for those of you hearing it for the first time as fresh revelation. In all that you discover and learn when praying for the sick, I want to encourage you to rely on, lean on, listen to, and follow the leading of the Holy Spirit.

CHAPTER 12

A CHAPTER FOR PARENTS
YOUR UNDIVIDED ATTENTION IS NEEDED!

I FELT COMPELLED TO WRITE THIS CHAPTER SPECIFICALLY because as you have made your way through the book you would have read over and over again how demons mostly enter us when we are children. Whether you are a parent or not, everyone knows that there is a fundamental responsibility to raise children in a loving, safe, secure, and moral environment, as well as making sure a child's physical needs are met. If we are Christians, then we will do our best to lead our children spiritually. That may be in the form of taking them to church, teaching them to pray, praying with them at night, having family Bible study, or it may be as simple as teaching them to say grace over their meals! I so wish I had the understanding I have now of how much the spiritual realm is a huge factor in the wellbeing and growth of our children. Had I known what I know now, leading my children spiritually would have been my number-one priority. That being said, I can honestly say with my children it was the grace of God that helped my husband

and I to raise all four of them to love God! It's always been a regular occurrence that people comment on how blessed they are when they see our children ministering and serving faithfully in the church. Now as adults, all four of them are in love with the Lord, and alongside my eldest son's wife, they all serve Him faithfully.

This is the thing, though—it's so easy to look at other people's families from the outside and presume everything is wonderful. I can tell you even though my children have been brought up in church from birth to grown adults in a loving, God-fearing family, they *still* had doors open in their lives for demons to attack them. As their parents, those doors opened through what we unknowingly allowed. It was our fault. (I will explain later in this chapter!) Whatever you believe is the correct way for raising a child spiritually, I want to show you something at the end of this chapter that I believe, if you are not already doing it, is essential, necessary, and vital for every parent to do. Before I get there, first I want to talk about a few other important matters.

I want to explain why parents hold the most significant role next to God in the life of their child or children. As God is the giver of all life, He has given us delegated responsibility to produce life after our kind. In Genesis 1:27-28 (NKJV) says:

> *So God created man in His own image; in the image*
> *of God He created him; male and female He created*
> *them. Then God blessed them, and God said to them,*
> *"Be fruitful and multiply; fill the earth and subdue*
> *it; have dominion over the fish of the sea, over the*

birds of the air, and over every living thing that moves on the earth."

By producing life, God has also given us delegated authority over that which we have given birth to. The authority is that of spiritual, physical, and emotional governance. The dictionary definition of *govern* says, "to rule over by right of authority, to exercise a directing or restraining influence over; guide; to hold in check; control." The synonyms of *governance* are to administer, manage, oversee, supervise, command, exercise authority, be in the driver's seat.

Parents are meant to lead their children in spiritual development and introduce them at the youngest age to their creator God and heavenly Father. They are also meant to nurture and guide their child emotionally and physically until the child becomes an adult and matures and grows in those areas so that they can live a godly, fruitful, and productive life. Parents are charged with protecting their children spiritually, physically, and emotionally. While most parents put the emphasis on the physical raising of their children, the spiritual and emotional part of protection is neglected, and this is where many of us fail because we don't pay enough attention to it.

The Bible says a child is a gift from God, and God expects us to take good care of what He has entrusted to us. The problems occur when parents have failed to protect a child at any point throughout their childhood spiritually and emotionally or when they have neglected their child's wellbeing physically. If a parent has abused a child in any way, the child will feel insecure, rejected, and afraid because the person or people with the delegated authority over them have abused that authority, yet without fail the child will feel the need to keep trying to get that care and attention they should have received from the parent, no matter what age they are.

It's hard for most of us to comprehend why an adult who may have suffered at the hands of an abusive parent would want to gain approval or love from them. The reason is that it's a spiritual tie. Parenthood is delegated spiritual authority over another human, and because it's spiritual, when any abuse or failure to protect a child occurs spiritually, emotionally, or physically, that negative attachment or spiritual soul tie can only be broken through the means of deliverance.

Having delegated spiritual responsibility over other humans (our children) is like walking around with a target on our back where the enemy is concerned. Satan makes it his mission to destroy our ability to do this well, starting at the conception of a child. Creating life in the womb can only be done with the seed of a male and the egg of a female. Even though scientists have gained the knowledge to produce the initial stages of life outside of the womb, they still cannot produce a fully formed human; they need the womb of a woman to grow a baby. Satan would love to be able to produce life the way that we do, but because he can't, he has continually tried to distort the God-given ability that we have. I should add at this point that in Genesis 6:2,4 we are told about the "sons of God" having intimacy with the daughters of men, and as already discussed in a previous chapter, the offspring of this union were the race of giants known as the Nephilim. We are not told what kind of created beings the "sons of God" were, but what we are told is that the women were human. Either way, they were God's

creation, and it was the male and female that produced life, albeit ungodly life.

I make this point because I want to touch on homosexuality, abortion, and transgenderism for one moment. All three attack and disobey God's command to us to be fruitful and multiply. Homosexuality is the easiest way to stop us from producing life. According to the word of God, it is an unnatural way for humans to be intimate with one another because it is neither sanctioned nor blessed by God. God gave the command to replenish the earth, which is impossible for a male and male to do as they cannot produce life. Neither can a female and female produce life. They do not physically fit together and so cannot have intercourse, which is the natural way for life to begin.

Another way Satan is influential is by convincing women that they are the ones who get to choose whether the life they carry in their womb should live or die, deceiving them into thinking there is no spiritual or moral consequence to their decision. Satan has fed women the lie that because it's their body, it's their choice! Satan never reveals the consequences of these choices, but there are always consequences when the choice you make is sinful.

To prevent men from producing life, he has deceived many men into believing they were born into the wrong body—that either God or science made a mistake and that they feel female; so now they want to identify as being women. The very thing that makes a man unique is his ability to produce a seed that can give life. Satan has deceived men into mutilating the very body parts that give them this ability. Likewise, he has deceived women in the same way, believing they too were born in the

wrong body. The transgender movement is a demonic movement distorting the originality and purpose of male and female. It's interesting that while transgenderism affects both males and females, the main attack is against females with males trying to dominate and replace women and their roles in every sphere of life. Satan has always hated women. From the moment he was cursed for deceiving Eve, God put enmity between Eve and the serpent in the garden:

> *And I will put enmity between you and the woman, and between your seed and her Seed; He shall bruise your head, and you shall bruise His heel* (Genesis 3:15 NKJV).

Enmity means "true hatred and hostility, either overt or concealed." No wonder the attack is so fierce against women. It's not anything new, it's just a different method of attack. Satan wants to wipe out women entirely from the planet. Remember what John 10:10 says—Satan only comes to steal, kill, and destroy, and he desperately purposes to do that to women.

Most people recognize that there is no scientific evidence or explanation to confirm transgenderism—it is literally an ideology, a wish list for deceived people, fooled by Satan. He has targeted men by selling them the idea that being a woman is dressing up, looking pretty, and being in touch with their emotions. It's such an attack and is nothing more than a concealed way to destroy a woman's identity and to emasculate a man.

Just a side note here—I think if any man had to endure menstruation cycles every month for 40-plus years, pregnancy and giving birth (which is like pushing a melon out of your

nostril!), followed by menopause, they would run a mile! I am a woman and have experienced every one of the above, and apart from pregnancy, none of it is pleasant!

Men *cannot* change to become women, and women *cannot* change to become men. It's scientifically, emotionally, and spiritually impossible, and at the end of the day whatever bits people choose to cut off or add, DNA will always bear witness to how God originally made them. Every person is one of two sexes, either male or female; there is no other gender that was created.

> *So God created man in His own image; in the image of God He created him; male and female He created them* (Genesis 1:27 NKJV).

The sex and gender of a person is decided by God before the foundation of the world, and they are not separate entities. He tells us who we are regardless of how we may feel on the inside:

> *For You formed my inward parts; You covered me in my mother's womb. I will praise You, for I am fearfully and wonderfully made; marvelous are Your works, and that my soul knows very well. My frame was not hidden from You, when I was made in secret, and skillfully wrought in the lowest parts of the earth. Your eyes saw my substance, being yet unformed. and in Your book they all were written, the days fashioned for me, when as yet there were none of them* (Psalm 139:13-16 NKJV).

This distortion of truth comes because Satan wants us to stop doing what we were uniquely created to do as male and female. It's one of the greatest attacks of them all, when you think about it. The very command that was given in the garden to multiply and replenish the earth has been distorted to the point that today, people genuinely question the definition of a man and woman! It's almost mind-blowing that this could even be a discussion, but Satan is so intent on destroying mankind that he will stop at nothing to advance his plan.

The deception that life is not precious and can be killed or wiped out with no consequence to us is a lie that is unrighteous and demonic! The very thing that God has blessed humanity with is the unique ability to produce life together, male and female coming together intimately to produce a baby. This has been devalued, despised, and disrespected, and if Satan could, he would destroy and irradicate our unique ability to do this.

Even with all his perversion and distortion, we know Satan doesn't have the power to destroy the seed of man or wipe out the woman. What he does instead is to try and cause as much harm as possible to the children who *are* born into this world. His primary mode of attack is using the parents to do it. Let me just make the point again of why a parent has so much power and influence over their child and why it's necessary for us to know and understand this. The reason why parents carry so much authority over their children is because the responsibility of their life has been delegated to them by God to watch over them spiritually, physically, and emotionally. When parents fail in any of these areas, the children suffer the consequences. Ultimately, God watches over them, but He expects parents who have this delegated authority and responsibility to look after their children as the gift they are.

Children are a gift from the Lord; they are a reward from him (Psalm 127:3 NLT).

When a gift is given, all rights pass to the person the gift is given to. It's almost difficult to comprehend that God would give us this amount of responsibility, but He trusts us to do the right thing with the gift He has given us. Most parents, as best as they can, whether Christian or not, do the right thing. Unfortunately, through the influence of demons or generational curses and destructive seeds sown, some parents don't take care of their children to the point of destroying the gift they have been entrusted with. It's so sad to witness the damage parents either knowingly or unknowingly can do to their children. The power an abusive parent has over a child is unparalleled, and we see the effects repeatedly in the ministry of deliverance. As the child grows and becomes an adult, they are ruled emotionally by the parent because of the abuse they have suffered at their hands, yet they will still try to seek approval, acceptance, and love from them.

You may be one of those people reading this. A parent who was abusive to you may still have an emotional hold over you that you can't shake free from even after all these years. You may no longer be in contact with them, but the emotional ties of the trauma are still there. I want to encourage you that there is freedom in Christ, and hopefully this chapter will provide some answers to why you still feel the way you do. My main hope is that you will gain an understanding of the spiritual aspects that have bound you to the relationship and the release that can come when you are delivered.

Protecting our children from the onslaught of the enemy should start when our babies are in the womb. What we speak over our unborn child in the womb is of the utmost importance. The environment we live in, our emotional state and wellbeing, and our mental health (especially of the mother) must be protected for the sake of having a healthy baby that is born emotionally and physically well:

> As a fetus [I would like to change this word to baby!] grows, it's constantly getting messages from its mother. It's not just hearing her heartbeat and whatever music she might play to her belly; it also gets chemical signals through the placenta. A new study, which will be published in Psychological Science, a journal of the Association for Psychological Science, finds that this includes signals about the mother's mental state. If the mother is depressed, that affects how the baby develops after it's born.
>
> …We believe that the human fetus [baby] is an active participant in its own development and is collecting information for life after birth. …It's preparing for life based on messages the mom is providing.[1]

This is something we have known for years. Everything can influence a baby while it's in the womb, and Satan knows it. He also knows that if the baby senses fear or hears violence and aggression while in the womb, it will make a significant impact throughout its life. This is why he will try to cause division, anger, and strife in relationships if he is permitted. When

the mother experiences stress, anxiety, depression, addictions of any kind, a troubled relationship with the father, etc., the baby will automatically be affected, and that's how spiritual doors are opened in the life of an innocent baby even before it takes its first breath in the world. When our babies are born, how we live as parents is vital for the life of our children. The environment we create in our homes as we are raising them will inevitably shape the course of their lives, whether it be good or bad. For some adults, living through a difficult or traumatic childhood has scarred them to the point that they struggle to feel they could ever live a normal life. They will often struggle in relationships and feel insecure in their identity throughout their entire life. It's hard to believe that this can all start because of the experience a baby has either in the womb or as a small child.

I want to give you some examples of adults who have needed deliverance because of their childhood, so that you know exactly what I'm talking about. It can be easy to look at other parents and think that they have got it all together and are raising their children in godly homes, but I must tell you that many people we deliver have come from Christian homes. Of course, there are extremes, which I will mention, but I will also give you examples that will show you how easily demons can gain access to our children in our homes if we are not aware of Satan's schemes. I want to alert all parents so that you have the information to kick the enemy out of your home today.

First, let me touch on this—something that is easy to ignore because it doesn't seem that important is the way the atmosphere in our homes can influence children growing up. Demons can gain and have access in the one place that is supposed to be a haven for children. We can all be excused for not understanding this fully before we were believers, but once you became born again you really have no excuse for allowing ungodly influences in your home. It may be difficult keeping the right atmosphere if you are the only parent who is born again, but as you pray, the Holy Spirit will instruct you as to what you should do to root out any evil influences that have crept in. It may not have occurred to you, but everything, from what you watch on TV to the music you play to objects that you have on your shelves or hanging on your walls, all influence young minds and the spiritual and emotional wellbeing of your children. If anything you are watching or listening to continually has themes of evil, horror, paganism, the occult, foul language, violence, sexual violence, or pornographic images, it will cause the atmosphere in your home to change. Your children will be influenced by it without having a say in the matter. Do demons enter your children because of this type of atmosphere? Probably not, but those demons will be present in your home, and the demons that have access in your home are just waiting for their opportune moment to enter your children. It only takes your child becoming fearful of what they are seeing or hearing.

I mentioned objects because some things we have in our homes are not just ornaments; they can be demonic or pagan symbols. Be sure that you know where and for what purpose things that you have in your home were made. Curses, pagan prayers, and spells are put on objects such as dream catchers, buddhas, Indian gods, crystals, and wood carvings. These can carry demon spirits with them, so it's always important with ornaments that you know what you are hanging or displaying in your home.

It gets a little more serious when the atmosphere in your home is full of constant arguing, aggression, fighting, outbursts of anger, even people you invite into your home. Any gossip or fault-finding can all potentially open the doors for demons to enter your home.

Children are the most vulnerable people in your home, and when they are consistently bombarded with any of the above, it starts to influence them in their hearts, even as babies and young children. You may think everything is going over their heads, but children have very tender hearts, and this kind of stuff makes an impact and impression on them that stays with them through life. When demons are at work in the parents, it is very easy for them to transfer to children when the heart of the child is full of fear, insecurity, or trauma.

What are you unknowingly exposing your children to? You may be asking yourself the question, "How will I know if my child already has been demonized?" Some of the signs, of course, will be dependent upon what is going on in your home, but generally your child may be aggressive or rebellious, tell lies, have overly sexualized tendencies, struggle in school to learn, will not listen, have constant temper tantrums, may become quiet and introverted, or will have constant feelings of insecurity. This is not an exhaustive list but are some of the main signs that we look out for when a child has demons.

This is the importance of our roles as parents that we protect our children from the youngest age and from every form of attack from the enemy. In my own personal case, two major things happened. The first happened to one of our daughters, who at the time was five years old, when we were disciplining her older brothers. She could hear the screaming coming from the next bedroom. Let me add here that our boys were typically boisterous and would never go to sleep when they were supposed to. It wasn't a case of us hurting them. In fact, by the time we got close enough to punish them they would scream so loudly that we would crack up laughing. However, all my daughter heard were the loud screams, and that caused fear to enter her little heart. For years, she struggled to sleep and would have night terrors, and it was only recently that she was delivered from the demon that entered her all that time ago.

In hindsight, when she was afraid, we should have prayed with her and rebuked any fear that was trying to come on her, but we just didn't know about this kind of stuff back then. The other thing that happened was when we allowed our youngest son at the age of 11 years old to sleep over at a friend's house. We didn't even think about it and just let him carry on without checking the home he was going to. Unfortunately, his friend introduced him to pornography, which became an addiction that he struggled with for years. The spirit of addiction and pornography came into our home, which then affected our youngest daughter. What we now realize sadly is that as parents we had struggled with this in our own lives in the past, and so it wasn't our son who brought it into the home; it started with us. Praise God we are all delivered and set free from it, but the realization that Satan will attack our children with the very thing we as parents have struggled with should make us wake up, take control, and get delivered if necessary! We must be aware of all the spiritual activity both good and bad that is taking place in our homes.

A precious Christian lady came for prayer, who for years had struggled with the abuse she had suffered throughout her childhood. She could not move on from the pain and injustice of what she went through, and her life decisions as a result were not good, causing her to fall into addiction and numerous abusive relationships. Everything she did was rooted in the physical and emotional abuse she suffered at the hands of a Christian father who was a strict disciplinarian. He punished her and her siblings to the point of blood and bruises being visible on their bodies. While hating what happened to her as a child, this lady still sought approval, acceptance, and love from her father and even her mother, who at the time felt helpless to do anything about the abuse. It left her feeling abandoned and rejected. The saddest thing is that even though they were the cause of her abuse, they never accepted responsibility but blamed her for her own life choices. How sad that there are parents out there who deny the trauma they have caused their children, leaving them wide open to demonic attack and the need for deliverance.

For this lady, deliverance set her free from all the demons that had entered her when she was a child, as well as all the ones that had entered her as an adult because of the childhood demons. Her case is not unusual; I hear this type of story repeatedly. Most are so similar, and if it's not physical or emotional abuse, it's sexual abuse by a relative or friend who was allowed into the home unchecked by parents. I want to say here—please be aware of what is going on in your home. Your children are vulnerable, and Satan is wicked and evil.

A young Christian man who was verbally put down and emotionally abused by his father throughout his childhood and into his adulthood eventually got free once we had brought everything into the light. His father was violently abusive to his mother, which made him fearful but also filled him with hatred and anger toward his father. He was able to talk about his struggles of insecurity and of feeling rejected and abandoned, which had affected every relationship he had. He suffered with depression all his life, but through deliverance this spirit was cast out along with all the other spirits that had entered him from the abuse he had suffered as a child.

I just want to mention that for many Christian people who have been traumatized or abused in any way by a parent, they find it very difficult to come to terms with the scripture that commands us to honor our mother and father. It seems incredibly unfair to have to do this and to honor those who have abused us; however, the scripture comes with a promise of long life.

> *Honor your father and mother. Then you will live a long, full life in the land the Lord your God is giving you* (Exodus 20:12 NLT).

Jesus also repeated this commandment in the gospels. I have seen many people living awful lives because of the hate they have had for their parents. They just can't find it in their hearts to forgive them. Unforgiveness ties God's hands; He cannot fight on our behalf. Forgiveness cancels the debt and allows God to take vengeance on our behalf. If you find yourself in this position, draw on the power and the help of the Holy Spirit. He is your comforter, your strength, and will give you the ability to love. It's the only way you will be healed and delivered and fully set free.

Most of us as parents do our best to raise our children well, but you cannot just presume everything will be okay with them, especially because Satan has access to almost every child on the planet through mobile phones and social media. I'm not trying to frighten you as a parent and I'm not saying that your child is influenced by or has a demon; what I am saying is that Satan is after your children and that your responsibility as a parent is to spiritually take control in your home and, as much as possible, in the environments that your children are subject to.

Here are the keys that I believe are essential, necessary, and vital and that every parent should continually practice, ensuring your child is growing up in a healthy, God-influenced environment.

First, get yourself right. Do you need deliverance from past trauma, abuse, or addictions? If so, go to the chapter "Step by Step." Read it and then pray the prayer at the end of the chapter.

Second, do you think you have inadvertently given demons access to influence your children? If so, pray over your child's heart and mind (do this as often as you need to). Bind any spirits operating in your home or any trying to gain access to your child. If you know what spirits they are, then name them. Close any open doors you believe may have opened in your child's life by rebuking the enemy and using the name of Jesus. Remember, you have spiritual authority over your child, and because of this your prayers are very powerful; you can pray either with them or for them. Pray something like this:

Dear heavenly Father, I lift up (child's name) to You right now and in Jesus' Name I bind all spirits of (name them: anger, rebellion, pornography, division) trying to come into this home and into to my child. I close all doors that may have opened through what I have allowed into this home. Father, I repent right now, and I thank You for Your forgiveness. I pray peace that surpasses all understanding over (child's name)'s heart and mind right now, and I loose them from any activity or evil spirit that the enemy has bound them with in Jesus' Name, amen.

Third, if it's necessary and you realize that your child has been demonized, then you can deliver them by getting them to renounce all the ungodly, angry emotions that they are experiencing. Again, you can follow the prayer in the chapter "Step by Step"

Finally, keep the atmosphere in your home godly, wholesome, and strife-free. Know your authority and responsibility as a parent and pray peace and the joy of the Lord over the entire atmosphere of your home. Even if you have rebellious teenagers at home right now, you still have the final spiritual authority in your home because you are the parent and you have been given the delegated authority and responsibility by God. So, use it! Bind any or all spirits of rebellion in Jesus' Name! As you start to walk in your God-given authority, you will begin to see change in your child and in your home.

Note

1. A. Sandman, Elysia P. Davis, and Laura M. Glynn, qtd. in *ScienceDaily*, "Can fetus sense mother's psychological state? Study suggests yes," Association for Psychological Science, November 10, 2011, https://www.sciencedaily .com/releases/2011/11/111110142352.htm.

CHAPTER 13

FREE AT LAST
TESTIMONIES

MY SINCERE HOPE AS YOU READ THIS LAST CHAPTER OF THE book is that it will just make sense, that the penny will drop, and it has scratched the itch that you have never been able to reach! I am believing it has answered the questions that you have always been asking but could never resolve in your heart and mind. Ultimately, I am hoping this has helped you personally, especially if you have struggled in any of the areas discussed throughout this book. Be encouraged, there is hope and there is freedom!

So let me take this last opportunity to encourage you. Up until this point, you may have been convincing yourself that none of this affects you and that while you have enjoyed the book, it's not something that relates to you in the sense that you don't believe demons affect you! You may have been going back and forth in your mind, thinking about experiences you have had or emotions you have always struggled with, or you may have been having a conversation with yourself as to whether you have allowed demons entrance into your life. If your heart has beat faster during the reading of this book or you have

questioned yourself in any way, then I would say that it is a clear indication that demons are involved in some way, and it is necessary for you to pray!

If this is the case, I want to encourage you to do one of two things—either return to the chapter right now that has the prayer of deliverance or read to the end of this chapter and follow the instructions I have given. Listen! It's all good news— don't fret, don't worry. This is the best day of your life. It's revelation day, and fresh revelation of the living word applied has the power to change everything!

Giving testimony is a huge part of deliverance because it exposes the works of darkness, which demons hate! Demons thrive on doing everything in secret and in darkness, weaving their web of lies and deceit in our lives. Well, I want to finish off with some real-life testimonies that not only expose them but demonstrate the power of God and reveal the weakness of demons! These testimonies have changed lives forever, and they are living testaments to the power of God both in heaven and in hell.

> *Therefore God also has highly exalted Him and given Him the name which is above every name, that at the name of Jesus every knee should bow, of those in heaven, and of those on earth, and of those under the earth, and that every tongue should confess that Jesus Christ is Lord, to the glory of God the Father* (Philippians 2:9-11 NKJV).

I have chosen testimonies to share with you that I believe will really encourage you. Some of them are dramatic and may sound wild, but all of them have an outcome that has changed the person's life forever! I haven't given names on purpose, but I want to say, none of us is exempt from being demonized. Whoever you are, demons don't care what position you hold or how important you are. Pastors and leaders are targets for the enemy and are key people demons try to enter because they affect so many! I have personally delivered many people in pastoral and leadership positions, including some of my own family members.

It's a funny fact, but I'll start off with this one. I have been delivered myself as I have been delivering others! It's not just happened to me once either! The worst time, which was the first time, was at the very beginning of this new ministry God was giving me. It was with a young woman who was a member of our church at the time. She had been involved in the occult, had lots of abuse in her life growing up, and had had a lot of negative sexual encounters and addictions. I can remember having to duck several times during the deliverance as she was swinging out, screaming, and jumping all over the place. I called out a demon of sexual perversion and she started retching.

As this was happening, suddenly I felt sick like I could hardly stand up. I thought any moment I was going to faint. I had to excuse myself to go to the bathroom and let the others continue the deliverance without me. In the bathroom, I started retching over the sink. It lasted for about twenty seconds, and then it was all over and I felt normal again. I went back out and continued with the deliverance until the young woman got free! At the time I didn't think too much of it, I just thought it was a little strange, and after the deliverance we actually joked about it. I will say sometimes a demon's presence can be so strong and

potent that it can create that feeling of nausea for everyone in the room. Sometimes they even emit a terrible smell—neither of these are uncommon. However, after a few other times concerning other demons when I have coughed or burped (so embarrassing!), I recognized that I have gotten free of some unwanted guests myself. Most have been things I had experienced in my life growing up. It's a good thing it took place because I know I am free, but I regularly check myself now, along with our delivery team. Knowing how demons operate, we don't take anything at face value, and the moment the Holy Spirit nudges us about anything we may have let in, we make sure they are let out immediately!

One of the wildest deliverances I have encountered was a guy I first met when he became involved in our outreach team. He had only been saved for eight months, but he was so in love with the Lord. Before I continue, I just want to slip in here a protocol we have put in place—whenever I deliver men, I will always have either my husband with me or other male pastors who are trained in deliverance. This is mainly due to the nature of the conversation that is normally talked about during counseling, but also the spiritual covering that my husband gives me just by being there. With this particular guy, he was very tall and had tattoos that covered much of his body and his face. Just by the nature of the tattoos and the brief conversation I had with him, I knew my husband being there was the right call. We needed male authority—plus, my husband is strong!

When we sat down to have the conversation (the counseling part of the deliverance), he talked about the bullying and abuse he had suffered in the home as a child, which had continued through his teens in school and into adulthood. He had been violently attacked in the streets by unknown assailants, and his head had been kicked so much that it had left him with life-long facial injuries. He had become angry and aggressive and was continually bombarded in his mind with thoughts of how to hurt and kill people in the most violent ways he could imagine. In searching for answers to life, he became involved in the New Age movement. He learned how to astral project out of his body and travel into different times and spheres. He didn't have any idea that what he was involved in was demonic or had its roots in the occult and Satanism. Even though he had had such violent experiences in his life, as a person he was gentle. His personality was kind and caring, and he only stumbled on the New Age movement because he was searching for peace in his life, and he thought what he had found was good, loving, and peaceful.

Eventually, he realized that New Age wasn't the answer, and so continued his search. He heard the message of the gospel of how much God loved him and how He sent Jesus to die for him. It was what he was searching for, and so he accepted Jesus as his Lord and Savior. The moment he became born again, those New Age demons became furious. Every night they would manifest in his room. He would physically see them and feel them; they would attack him so violently that he would wake up every morning feeling that he had been murdered. He would feel the pain of the knife wounds they would inflict on his body. In his dreams the demons would also make him violently attack others. As he was attacking people, the demons would make him want to murder someone. As he was explaining all of this, he then added that he was an ex-MMA fighter!

I am so glad my husband was there. We had another pastor who was an ex-rugby player, so he was big guy, and then we also had our security guy who just wanted to sit in on the deliverance to learn! We do this when we are training people. We allow them to sit in and observe. So there were three guys and me! As normal, we went through the three things we require from the person being delivered: honesty, forgiveness, and desperation. We then moved on to the prayer, which he said with no problem at all. As he stood up, I knew things were about to get interesting. He towered over the rest of us. As he renounced the demons that had been harassing him—trauma, bullying, violence, aggression, rage, murder, hate—I commanded that every demon attached to what he had renounced had to leave and come out in Jesus' Name. The moment I finished commanding this, his whole body went as stiff as a board. He started leaning forward and went into a trance-like state. The guys were holding him up, and at that point I looked over to our security guy who was just observing. With my eyes I communicated that we needed him ASAP. At the same time, my husband was signaling with his head, "We need you!" Then suddenly it was like there was an explosion in the room. He screamed so loud, his jaw opened to almost the size of his face. He threw everyone to the ground, his arms and legs flailing all over the place! The guys managed to grab an arm or a leg and hold him down, but he started banging his head on the floor swearing, screaming, and spitting! I'm not kidding, it was loud, and it was a baptism of fire in the deliverance ministry for our security guy!

One thing I will say—demons aren't deaf, so you don't have to shout louder than everyone else in the room for them to come

out. You must be assertive and forceful, yes, but you should never be exhausted from deliverance through yelling! I learned this the hard way in the early days of delivering people. I would constantly lose my voice from all the shouting and commanding them out! The order of who is leading any kind of deliverance is extremely important. When everybody is yelling at the demons, they determine that no one is in charge, and when everyone is calling out everything, you will not know what has left and what has stayed. Demons will use this to their advantage.

I had not really discussed this with the guys before the deliverance and so, faced with a violent, aggressive person who was trying to attack us, everyone was commanding all sorts of things to come out very loudly, all at once, and for a few moments the whole thing was chaotic. If anyone had been outside the doors hearing what was going on, they would have called the police. After what seemed like forever, the guys managed to stop him banging his head on the floor and fighting them, and just through sheer exhaustion he stopped and calmed down. When he sat up, it was clear some things had left, but he was physically and emotionally exhausted. (So were we!) I explained to him that he would need to come back for more deliverance.

As it happened, the following day we were at the church training pastors and leaders in the deliverance ministry. He turned up and said he had had the worst night ever and that huge demons had attacked him as he tried to sleep. I agreed that he needed to receive deliverance that day, but we had a roomful of people just learning about this stuff and they were not ready to be involved in his deliverance, plus I didn't want to give those demons an audience to perform to!

For about ten minutes he sat in the group as I was training them, but his face looked like he wanted to kill someone. My husband spotted this and so took him out for a coffee until the training was over. The further away he got from the church, the calmer he became, and my husband was able to minister the word to him for a good hour before he brought him back. This time we were prepared, plus we added an extra guy, our head host, who happened to be super strong! I went through the prayer once again, had him renounce all the demons, and then just like the night before, he went into the trance-like state.

Without warning, this time he went for my husband and tackled him to the floor. All the guys managed to pull him off and hold on to his arms and legs. He was screaming, spitting, and swearing once again, banging his head on the floor, but now he was trying to bite everyone. With authority this time, I was able to speak so that the demons could hear me. Between me and my husband we commanded them to stop hurting him, which they did. I commanded them to leave him completely, and within twenty minutes, after much screaming and protesting from the demons, they left. The atmosphere was incredible. The Holy Spirit flooded us, and we all just sat there on the floor in silence, marveling at the awesomeness of God. He couldn't stop crying, his face was full of joy, and for the first time in his life he felt peace.

Suffice it to say, I learned a lot from that deliverance. If I deliver anyone who has been involved in the occult in any way, shape, or form, I will bind those demons straightaway from "performing" or trying to lash out violently at anyone (including me) or even the person being delivered. Many times, they

will make a point of trying to injure the person they are inhabiting, especially if it's a spirit of self-harm or suicide. I will also command them to come out quietly! I realized that if you don't take authority or charge of the situation straightaway, then the demons will try and control what is happening in the room.

A fascinating deliverance was a lady who had joined our church wanting more of the move of the Holy Spirit. She was a very large lady and had struggled with her weight since childhood. There were many other things that she spoke about during the conversation, but it came out that obesity had played a huge part in her life and had plagued her from a little girl. It had run in all the women in her family, and she could never remember a time when she wasn't hungry. Throughout her adult life, she had tried every diet known to man. She was always on some kind of diet. She would lose weight but then gain more once she stopped the diet. It was a constant yo-yo effect with eating, dieting, losing weight, gaining weight, eating, dieting.

As we started to pray, we called out demons of low self-esteem, comparison, and a few others, which came out quietly, but it was only when we called the demon of obesity out that she let out the mightiest shriek that lasted for what felt like an eternity. My ears almost popped, it was that loud and piercing! It was amazing to watch because I could see her get visibly free! At the time I didn't realize it, but it was evident that this was the strongman, the demon that had first entered her as a small girl. It didn't just start with her—this was a generational curse, something that had traveled down from her mother's side. When the demons are hereditary, they really don't want to leave because they feel they have a right to be there since they have "owned" the family for such a long time. It's one of the most important things we do in deliverance because we are breaking demonic control in a family line that can be decades or even centuries old!

When people get delivered, there should always be an instant change in their demeanor. We expect it immediately, for reasons that I explained in previous chapters, but when you see a sudden physical change it's the most incredible thing to witness! Within a month, this lady had lost over 50 pounds in weight! It was amazing to see, and we give God all the glory for the miraculous changes that occurred both on the inside and outside of her! To know Satan keeps people in such bondage makes you want to go and cast demons out of every single person who struggles in this area. Obviously, not every weight problem is a demon, and you can't cast a demon of lack of self-control out because it's not a demon! But in this case, it was a demon of obesity, and it had no choice but to leave even after thirty-plus years of tormenting her!

Most deliverances go the way we expect in the order of how we do things, but sometimes people are that worked up before they come, they only just manage to get in the building before the demons start manifesting. When the person has already made their decision that they want to get free, the demons know this and so will try and do everything within their power to stop them coming to the church. It varies, but generally people will feel nausea, or they will have a headache. They will feel anxious, nervous, or sweaty. Sometimes as they drive around the corner onto the road that our church is on, they will feel sick to their stomachs. One lady managed to get into the deliverance room, but she couldn't stand up or even sit down. When we walked into the room, she was stretched out over the sofa and couldn't string any words together. Obviously, there was no way we were able to go through our usual order of deliverance, and so straightaway we had to command those demons that were restricting her to get out. Once they were out and she was able to sit up and speak, we were then able to carry on the deliverance as normal.

There was one lady, who came to us from another church, whose background was particularly traumatizing. She was abused physically and sexually as a little girl, which then carried on with the abuse of one of her own children by a partner. She had tried everything from counseling to doctors and medication, but nothing could wipe out all the trauma she had been through and was still going through. She struggled with continuous sickness in her bowel and stomach area, which stemmed from abuse she received as a child, resulting in medical intervention all her life. Among all the other demons, we called out the spirit of infirmity. She was a gentle, quiet lady and was small in height, but oh my goodness the strength she had when we started calling those demons out was that of ten men! The demons were fierce, aggressive, and extremely angry with her for exposing them and wanting them gone! They did everything they could to stay. It was a very physical deliverance. The demons were trying to attack her by scratching her arms and face using her own hands to do the damage. It took all our strength to hold her and even then, she came away with scratches on the one side of her arm, face, and neck. Demons are very strong, and when they are being cast out, they will use

all their weight to stay! Of course, they can't stay if they are renounced; they must leave. In this lady's case, these demons, as much as they performed, could not stay.

It was the most amazing deliverance though and one I will always remember because of the instant joy and laughter that she had the moment the last demon left! You could feel the love the Father had for her, and the tangible presence of the Holy Spirit in the room was overwhelming. A couple of days later she contacted us to say that the doctors had called to say they couldn't believe it, but they didn't think she would need any more medical intervention. I love the fact that physical healing and deliverance can go hand in hand!

Another lady who came to us didn't even know she needed deliverance until she responded to an altar call in one of our services. I happened to be speaking on deliverance and how demons can enter through no fault of our own due to experiences that have happened in our past. When I mentioned that doors can open in our life through all forms of abuse, she knew she needed to receive prayer. One of our female pastors, who is also part of the deliverance team, started to pray with her, and for the first time in her life, as a 40-year-old women, she confessed that she had been sexually abused as a child. As she spoke it out, she sobbed uncontrollably. It was a secret that was buried so far down that she never thought she would ever be able to speak of it. No one knew; she had never told a soul, not even her husband. Her marriage had suffered greatly because of it, but in that moment as the pastor called out the spirits of abuse and trauma, she experienced the biggest release from such a huge burden of trauma that she had carried all her life. Through extra

counseling with both her and her husband and more deliverance prayer, she got completely free!

All these testimonies are from believers; deliverance for the believer is a real thing. I have seen way too much to be convinced otherwise. I have prayed with good, godly people who are sold out for Jesus and who love Him. I have prayed for pastors and leaders; I have prayed for the young and the old, men and women, and I have prayed for my own family. All have received deliverance that has changed their lives forever. Understanding and living the John 10:10 life is not just a hope; it has become reality for many as they have been delivered and set free.

For those of us who have been demonized, it has happened without us even realizing it, but my hope is that this book has brought clear understanding of this subject and a way forward for you, your loved ones, your children, and your friends.

I know deliverance for the saints is necessary so that we can run our race, live the abundant life, walk unhindered, have clarity of mind, and ultimately be completely free in our body and soul!

If you believe you need deliverance, then this is relevant to you. Be humble and bold enough to do something about it. Pray this prayer with me.

> *Holy Spirit, reveal to me those demons that have gained entrance into my life.*

Wait for the Holy Spirit to reveal them to you, then continue to pray.

> *In the Name of Jesus I renounce the spirits of (name*

them) _____,

_____.

You no longer have any authority to be in my life.
I rebuke you and loose myself from you; I command
every one of you to leave me now—out now, in
Jesus' Name.

Now that you have prayed this prayer, I want to encourage you to find a trusted pastor, leader, friend, or deliverance minister who can help you get completely free if you feel you need extra help. Please know that just by saying this simple prayer with authority in Jesus' Name, whatever you renounced must obey you! Remember how the disciples in Luke 10 were so excited that the demons obeyed them. It's the same for you and me—they will obey because they must obey the believer.

Be encouraged—we all have the authority to live in freedom!

Behold, I give you the authority to trample on
serpents and scorpions, and over all the power of the
enemy, and nothing shall by any means hurt you.
Nevertheless do not rejoice in this, that the spirits are
subject to you, but rather rejoice because your names
are written in heaven (Luke 10:19-20 NKJV).

And He said to them, "Go into all the world and
preach the gospel to every creature. He who believes
and is baptized will be saved; but he who does not
believe will be condemned. And these signs will
follow those who believe: In My name they will cast
out demons; they will speak with new tongues; they
will take up serpents; and if they drink anything

deadly, it will by no means hurt them; they will lay hands on the sick, and they will recover" (Mark 16:15-18 NKJV).

ABOUT DONNA HOWELLS

Donna Howells lives in South Wales, UK. Along with her husband Robbie, she pastors The Warehouse Church, as well as co-hosting their weekly television program called *Taking You Forward* which airs on The Victory Channel and God TV.

Donna is a gifted teacher with an ability to help people understand some of the weightier messages of the word, including understanding the need for deliverance within the church.

FIND **DIRECTION**
FIND **PURPOSE**
FIND *Hope*

ONE CHURCH, THREE LOCATIONS

NEWPORT, WALES, UK **FARO, PORTUGAL**

PHOENIX, ARIZONA, USA

WWW.THEWAREHOUSECHURCH.TV

JOIN US IN PERSON OR ONLINE

THE WAREHOUSE CHURCH

YOUR HOUSE OF
FAITH

Sign up for a **FREE** subscription to the
Harrison House digital magazine and get
excellent content delivered directly to your inbox!

harrisonhouse.com/signup

Sign up for Messages that Equip You to Walk in the Abundant Life

- Receive biblically sound and Spirit-filled encouragement to focus on and maintain your faith
- Grow in faith through biblical teachings, prayers, and other spiritual insights
- Connect with a community of believers who share you values and beliefs

Experience Fresh Teachings and Inspiration to Build Your Faith

- Deepen your understanding of God's purpose for your life
- Stay connected and inspired on your faith journey
- Learn how to grow spiritually in your walk with God